ANGELS AT YOUR SERVICE

RELEASING THE POWER OF HEAVEN'S HOST

ANGELS AT YOUR SERVICE

RELEASING THE POWER OF HEAVEN'S HOST

by
Mac Hammond

Harrison House
Tulsa, Oklahoma

Unless otherwise indicated, all Scripture quotations are taken from the *King James Version* of the Bible.

Scripture quotations marked (AMP) are taken from *The Amplified Bible, New Testament*. Copyright © 1954, 1958, 1987 by the Lockman Foundation, La Habra, California. Used by permission.

Direct quotations from the Bible appear in bold type.

05 04 03 02 01   11 10 9 8 7

Angels At Your Service
Releasing the Power of Heaven's Host
ISBN 1-57794-059-8
Copyright © 1998 by Mac Hammond
P. O. Box 29469
Minneapolis, MN 55429

Published by Harrison House, Inc.
P. O. Box 35035
Tulsa, OK 74153

Contents

Angels All Around Us
• • •

As a recent writer in the Washington Post put it, "We are in the midst of an extraordinary boom of interest in angels."

According to *Publishers Weekly*, more than 100 new nonfiction books about angels appeared in one publishing season recently. Scores of angel sites have surfaced on the Internet and three glossy national magazines devoted exclusively to angels recently began publishing.

You can now purchase a book that claims to teach you how to consult your angels on investing, home improvement and how to cook a great dinner. There are books on how to harness your "angel energy." Books that turn angels into fortune-tellers and financial counselors. Books that teach you to look for angels in floating feathers, tinkling bells and passing pigeons. And if you need to drop a few pounds, "The Angel's Little Diet Book" is your ticket to a heavenly waistline.

This would all be amusing if the implications weren't so serious.

You see, there's just one problem with this avalanche of angel-ology. Most of it is at odds with the only reliable source on angels we have—the Bible. The good news is,

God's Word has quite a lot to say on the subject. In fact, the word *angel* appears more than 300 times in the Bible.

Until recently, many Americans never considered angels to be anything more than an image to be fanned in the snow, baked into sugar cookies, or perched atop the Christmas tree. But today, an explosion of interest in angels has forced Americans to consider the reality of these beings that have been written about for millennia.

In a 1996 Gallup survey, 55 percent of those polled said angels are higher beings created by God. Fifteen percent believed angels are people who have died. And 23 percent said angels are merely religious symbols.[1] Needless to say, there is a broad diversity of opinion about angels.

Yes, over the past fifteen years, there has been an astounding increase in people's curiosity about angels—not just in religious circles, but in the secular world as well. Never before have people been as interested in any spiritual subject as they currently are about angels. The proliferation of literature about angels and demons and the realm of the spirit they inhabit, reveals that these days almost everyone, whether religious or not, is fascinated with the supernatural.

SIGNS OF THE TIMES
• • •

This increased fascination with spiritual beings may seem remarkable when you first think about it. But actually, it isn't so remarkable if you consider the day in which we live. We are in the final days of this age. We are living in the generation that is going to usher in the millennial reign of the Lord. And already we are witnessing many biblically predicted signs that indicate the time is near. The most significant of these is the reestablishment of the nation of Israel.

History records that after Jesus was crucified, intense persecution came upon the church in Jerusalem. The persecution was so severe that it scattered the Jewish Christians throughout the world. Then in 70 A.D., the Roman emperor leveled Jerusalem and massacred anyone who was remaining.[2] For almost nineteen hundred years after that, the Jewish people had no homeland. Then an amazing—in fact, a miraculous—thing happened. In 1948, the international community recognized the sovereignty of Israel as a nation, and Jewish people from all over the world began to return to their homeland.

What does that mean to those of us who watch for Jesus' Second Coming? A lot! In Mark 13:30, Jesus proclaimed that the generation which witnessed the regathering of Israel (a process that began in 1948 and has been continuing ever since) *won't die*: **Verily I say unto you, that this generation shall not pass, till all these things be done.** *We* are that generation!

The Bible states clearly that no man will know the exact day or hour of the coming of the Lord. (Mark 13:32.) However, it also says that day shouldn't take us by surprise. (1 Thessalonians 5:4.) If we are alert to the scriptural signs, the Bible says we will know when Jesus' return is near.

As far as I'm concerned, there is no doubt about it. The signs are all around us. We are the generation that will see the close of this age and witness the establishment of Jesus' millennial reign.

It is so thrilling to think about that reign and the age to come. In that day, God will bring His kingdom, the realm of the Spirit, into contact with this natural, temporal earth. Then Jesus will literally and physically set up His earthly reign.

As we move closer towards that time, we will see more and more manifestations of the spiritual realm. Appearances of the angelic host, the seraphim and the cherubim and a variety of different angels will be increasingly commonplace in our generation.

DON'T BELIEVE EVERYTHING YOU HEAR
. . .

It shouldn't surprise us that people are starting to talk about these events or that there are so many reports about angels. In the coming days, we can expect secular newspapers and magazines to publish an increasing number of reports about people's encounters with angels. There will be television specials about them, and more books will be written about them.

Certainly, those things will be exciting to hear and read about, but we must be discerning. It is important to remember that not everything we hear through these sources will be accurate. In fact, much of the information that will be promoted will be deceptive and even dangerous.

The reason for all this erroneous information is very simple. Even though angels are real and the realm they inhabit is real, the human intellect alone can't understand them. Why? Because our minds have been created primarily to accommodate our needs in this earthly world. Our minds, in and of themselves, aren't spiritual. Thus, on our own, we simply don't have the capacity to properly interpret the spiritual manifestations that are becoming more and more commonplace.

If you want proof, just look a little closer at the results of the 1996 Gallup poll mentioned previously. They reveal the extremely inaccurate assumptions many people have made about the spiritual realm. The only good news in this study is the finding that despite how technologically advanced and sophisticated we like to think we are, seven out of ten Americans *do* believe in angels. The bad news is, of those seven who believe in angels, 50 percent believe only in "good" angels. They don't believe there is an evil angelic host. They believe that angels, by definition, are good and are sent by God to bring blessing to those who are in need.

Furthermore, 55 percent of those polled said they believe angels are a higher order of being (meaning higher than human beings) created by God. Fifteen percent of those polled believe that angels are people who have died and somehow acquired harps and wings. Twenty-three percent of those polled believe angels hold an important, symbolic place in a variety of religious persuasions but that they probably aren't real. Finally, 7 percent of those polled simply believe that angels are figments of the human imagination.[3]

What makes this study so significant? Two things. First of all, it reveals that this isn't just a "fringe" topic of study. This isn't something of interest to only a small minority of people because the majority of Americans believe in, and have some degree of interest in, angels.

Second, this survey demonstrates that ignorance about angels and the realm of the spirit is almost universal. It amazes me how little most people know about the subject. There are some people, I'm sure, who are well-versed in this area. However, the vast majority—Christians included—don't know as much as they should know about the mission and mandate of angels.

How can we solve this problem? How can we gather more accurate information about angels? By studying the only reliable resource we have—the Bible.

The Word as Our Guide
• • •

You can't discern spiritual truth with your natural senses. Therefore, anything you hear or read that doesn't originate from the Word of God has to be the opinion of man and, as such, should be taken with a grain of salt.

For that reason, it is my purpose to approach the subject of angels with the Bible as the final word on the subject. In the chapters that follow, we will look into the Word of God to define *who* angels are, *how* they were created, for *what* purpose they were created, what their capabilities and capacities are and how we are to relate to them. With the Word as our guide, we will be better able to judge encounters angels have with people. We will also come to understand the role angels play in the realization of our eternal destiny and our life on this earth.

Please understand that this book isn't meant to simply satisfy your curiosity about angels. It is meant to help you understand what God created them to do for you. How important is it to have this understanding? Well, let me put it this way. After studying what the Bible says about the subject, I'm firmly convinced that if you don't understand and draw upon the ministry of angels, it is unlikely that you will ever realize God's highest purpose for your life. Without the ministry of angels, you will probably never experience the fullness of His blessing or the magnitude of the destiny He has planned for you. It is that important.

As Christians, all of us need a greater revelation of the ministry of angels if we are to be used in the way God wants to use us. It is my hope that this book will open the door to that thrilling revelation and help us to better see the role angels can play in our lives.

A Little Lower Than . . .
•••

If we are to relate properly to the ministry of angels, the first thing we must understand is where they fit in God's order of things and what position they hold. This is important because their place in the kingdom of God helps identify our place in His kingdom as well. We need to know where *they* stand in order to know where *we* stand.

Now here is some potentially startling news in that regard. In God's hierarchy of created beings, angels hold a *lower* position than that of man. I realize that this may be difficult to accept, but the fact is that your role in God's scheme of things is actually elevated above that of angels. The Word of God is clear on this. Hebrews 2:5 AMP says: **For it was not to angels that God subjected the habitable world of the future, of which we are speaking.**

That is a very definite statement, isn't it? It declares that God hasn't put the world to come in subjection to angels. Rather, it has been placed in subjection to someone else. To whom then? Read Hebrews 2:6-8 in *The Amplified Bible*, and you will see.

> **It has been solemnly and earnestly said in a certain place, What is man that You are mindful of him, or the son of man that You graciously and**

helpfully care for and visit and look after him? For some little time You have ranked him lower than and inferior to the angels; You have crowned him with glory and honor and set him over the works of Your hands, for You have put everything in subjection under his feet.

God hasn't put the world to come in subjection to angels but to mankind—to you and me. He has put all things under *our* feet. We are the ones who have been set over the works of God's hand. That is our created destiny.

At first glance, that seems to contradict what we read in verse 7: **Thou madest him a little lower than the angels....** Why would we be lower than the angels if we are the ones who are going to exercise authority over God's creation? Conceptually, it doesn't seem possible, but a deeper look into the text solves this problem.

A DIFFERENT WORD FOR ANGEL
• • •

This dilemma is resolved when you read the passage in the Old Testament that the writer of Hebrews is quoting in verse 7. The passage is Psalm 8:5. If you want to fully understand this New Testament reference, it would be beneficial to have a clearer understanding of what the psalmist meant in that passage since it is being quoted here almost directly.

In Psalm 8:5, the English word *angel* has been given as the translation for the Hebrew word *Elohim*. Interestingly enough, this is the only place in the Bible that this word is translated *angel*. There is a different Hebrew word for angel that is used more than one hundred times in Old Testament writings. *Elohim*, on the other hand, is the word that is normally translated *God*. It is the Hebrew plural word for God, and it is always used in reference to the Godhead.

For example, *Elohim* is used repeatedly in the creation account in the first chapter of Genesis: **And God said** and thus **God made** (vv. 3,7). Later on in the chapter it reads, **And God said, Let us make man in our image, after our likeness** (v. 26). The expression **our image** indicates the plurality of the Godhead, and the Hebrew word for God in that verse is *Elohim*. It refers to the Trinity: God the Father, God the Son and God the Holy Ghost.

It is this same word that is used in Psalm 8:5. It literally says that man has been made a little lower than *Elohim*, and it is referring to the Godhead, not an angel.

TEMPORARILY INFERIOR BUT ETERNALLY SUPERIOR
• • •

In all fairness to the original translators, however, I do acknowledge that while we are on this earth, we are in a corruptible body, and our physical and intellectual capacities are comparatively less than those of angels. As a matter of fact, that may well be the intended meaning behind Hebrews 2:7 as some translations read: **a little inferior to angels** (Darby).[1] In other words, we are considerably limited in our capabilities while in this present condition.

As a matter of fact, I remember reading somewhere that the average human being uses only about 20 percent or less of the capacity of his brain. What the other 80 percent of the human brain is supposed to do or why it isn't being used is a mystery. Personally, I believe the fact that such a low percentage of the human brain is utilized relates to the fall of man. Man could no longer be entrusted with supernatural capabilities after he sinned and was separated from God. As a result, he lost many of his original abilities and giftings.

On the other hand, angels have access to the complete realm of the spirit. They are unhindered by sin. They aren't bound by space and time, and they are stronger and more intelligent than we are. Obviously, we are inferior to the angelic hosts in these areas.

But don't confuse that with God's creative purposes or your divinely appointed destiny. You are the creation made a little lower than God, in His image and His likeness, and He has given you dominion over this creation. God has put all things under your feet. As long as you are in a mortal body, you will be temporarily below angels in supernatural abilities. But never forget that you are eternally superior. Through Jesus, you are a son of God!

The appointed day will come when we, as believers, will exchange our mortality for immortality. We will trade our present, corruptible bodies for our new, glorified bodies. We will no longer be bound by the limitations of this temporal earth. At that time, according to 2 Corinthians 5:4, our mortality will be **swallowed up of life**. We will reign with Jesus as kings and even be called upon to judge the angels. (1 Corinthians 6:3.) Thus, we see the divine order as follows: God, man and angels.

When you read about God's creative order and purpose, always remember: You are second behind God the Father, God the Son and God the Holy Ghost. You have been created to rule with Him for an eternity over the vastness of this universe. That is *your* divinely appointed destiny—not the destiny of angels.

Touched by an Angel
•••

Now that we know where the angelic host fits in God's order of things, we need to examine the purpose of angels. We need to understand how the fulfillment of their destiny relates to our own eternal destinies. In short, we must ask, "Why were angels created, and what are they supposed to be doing?"

The answer to those questions is found at the end of the first chapter of Hebrews, where angels are identified as **ministering spirits, sent forth to minister for them who shall be heirs of salvation** (v. 14). That means you. You are an heir of salvation if you are born again and are in Christ. In fact, the Bible says you are a joint-heir with Jesus. (Romans 8:17.) Therefore, the angels have one purpose. They are sent forth to minister for you, both in the present time and in the eternal hereafter.

The Greek word translated *minister* is actually *diakonian*, and it literally means "to do service."[1] In other words, the angelic host has been commissioned to serve you. You ought to be excited about that, especially when you realize just how great a destiny God has prepared for you.

Once you understand the purpose of angels, the various testimonies you hear about them begin to make perfect sense. In virtually every instance, the testimonies are the same: an angel intervenes in the normal course of somebody's life to rescue them from disaster. Let me share with you several accounts that I found to be most interesting.

The Angel on Ice
. . .

The first account transpired in New Jersey and was reported in a national publication.

As I recall, two construction divers were working on a bridge. It was wintertime, and they were using special cold-water wet suits and other cold-weather equipment. They had just finished their day, and one of the two divers, a man named Nelson, threw all of his gear into the back of his truck.

Nelson said later he usually didn't do that. He normally put all of his gear into his locker at the construction site. But he said for some reason he threw it in the back of his truck that particular night.

As the two divers were driving home, they noticed a number of rescue vehicles pulled over to the side of the road. It was obvious there was some problem, and they were curious about what it was. So they pulled over to the side of the road to see.

Not far from the road was a large pond that had iced over. There was a hole in the ice near the center and, apparently, someone had fallen through. They quickly learned that it was a seven-year-old boy. He had been playing on the ice.

Rescue efforts for the boy had been hindered because a creek ran through the pond. Not only did the creek make the ice unstable, the current had swept the boy downstream and under the ice. He was no longer directly beneath the hole. The people who had gathered around the pond, including the rescue teams, were not able to find him.

Without hesitating, Nelson ran back to the truck and began to put on his wet suit and diving gear. He then ran back to the pond and dove down through the hole in the ice.

As soon as he got into the water, he realized the gravity of the situation. The water was so murky, he couldn't see his hand in front of his face. The strong current could have swept the boy's body anywhere. Nelson would never be able to see it.

Knowing the search was hopeless, he reluctantly returned to the surface to give the bad news to those who were waiting. But when he broke through the ice and looked out across the pond, Nelson saw a man standing twenty-five to thirty yards away from the hole. The man was some distance away from the crowd, and although everyone else wore heavy winter coats, this man was wearing a light, pastel-colored windbreaker. He was tall and had blonde hair.

Nelson looked at the man and saw him point to a spot on the ice beneath his feet. "Immediately, I thought that somebody had located the boy and this man was showing me where he was," Nelson said.

Diving back into the water, Nelson swam to the place where the man was pointing and discovered the boy. He brought the boy back to the hole in the surface and handed him to the rescue team.

Now, when someone, particularly a child, is submerged in extremely cold water, something happens to the cardio-vascular system and brain. It goes into a suspended state so that often an individual can be revived even after being submerged for long periods of time. Consequently, the rescue workers were able to completely resuscitate the boy, and he is fine today.

After the boy had been pulled out of the water, Nelson looked around for the man who had pointed out the boy's location. When he began to inquire about the man, he discovered that no one had seen anybody in a light, pastel-colored windbreaker. The man with the blond hair simply could not be found.

Because Nelson had a Christian background, he quickly assumed he had witnessed an angelic visitation and intervention on behalf of this young boy.

Several days later, Nelson visited the boy in the hospital. He brought the boy a small figurine of an angel as a gift because he was convinced that an angel was the reason the boy had survived. When Nelson gave him the figurine, the boy looked up at him and matter-of-factly said, "Thank you for this gift. An angel visited me yesterday in my room here and told me that he was glad that I was alive."[2]

A SPECIAL STRANGER
. . .

Now let me relate another account that appeared in a well-known news magazine about a woman named Mrs. Kennedy. According to the magazine report, Mrs. Kennedy had been diagnosed with a certain type of cancer and given only a year to live. Because this type of cancer produced tremendous suffering and pain, the doctors warned Mrs. Kennedy that her remaining year of life would be terribly difficult both for her and for her loved ones.

Mrs. Kennedy was a Christian who went to a traditional, mainline church and had never been taught much
about healing. After the report of her cancer, she had cried
out to God in prayer, "Lord, I don't want my husband to
go through that kind of year. If I have to die, just let me
die now."

The doctors had scheduled her for exploratory surgery
the next day on the off chance that they might be able to
prolong her life and catch the cancer before it spread. That
morning at her home, there was a knock at the door. Mrs.
Kennedy opened the door and found a tall, black man
standing on her porch.

She said he was as dark as anyone she had ever seen, yet
he had bright blue eyes. Her husband is six foot and five
inches, and, according to Mrs. Kennedy, this man towered
over him. The man introduced himself as Thomas and asked
if he could come in. Under normal circumstances, the
Kennedys wouldn't have invited a total stranger into their
home. But Mrs. Kennedy related later, "There was
something so special about this man's presence that my
husband and I agreed we should let him in."

Once inside, Thomas gave them a simple message: "God
said, 'By the stripes of Jesus, you are healed.'" He then held
out his hand to Mrs. Kennedy but didn't touch her. She said
she felt intense heat as his hand neared her forehead. She
then became unconscious and fell to the floor.

When she woke up some time later, Thomas had
departed and, of course, you can guess the rest of the story.
She went to the hospital the next day for her scheduled
surgery, and the doctors could find no cancer, although they
spent two days looking for it.[3]

DIVINE INTERVENTION
• • •

I remember reading yet another account of angelic activity about four people who were returning from a church meeting. They were in a car together on their way home. They had just come to the crest of a hill when, suddenly, a car that was totally out of control swerved into their lane.

According to their report, the oncoming car was estimated to be traveling over one hundred miles an hour, and was headed straight toward their car. There was no time to do anything to avoid the collision.

The account of each of the four passengers is identical. The driver cried out, "Jesus, save us!" and the next thing they knew, their car was slowing to a stop on the side of the road. There were no skid marks or screeching of tires. They simply drifted to a stop.

It is the driver's belief that an angel (or angels plural) had lifted up their car, and the runaway car had passed beneath them. Then their car was set gently back on the ground and came to a stop. Whatever happened, it was clearly a supernatural deliverance.

THE CHRISTIAN CONNECTION
• • •

These types of accounts are everywhere. And in all of them, one common element becomes apparent: an angel or a group of angels will manifest and invade this realm in order to bring deliverance or administer aid to a Christian or to someone whom a Christian knows and has prayed for.

There is always a Christian link or connection in these various testimonies.

If you will think back to Hebrews 1:14, you will see why. Angels are ministering spirits sent forth to minister for those who are the heirs of salvation. As Christians, you and I are the heirs of salvation. We are the ones who have been made a little lower than God, in His image, and He has put all things under our feet.

Angels are sent forth on our behalf, and all of the accounts and testimonies that I have ever read bear out this one simple truth.

Deliverance or Judgment?
•••

Unfortunately, most Christians have a casual knowledge of angels. But if they really want to experience the full benefit of the ministry of angels, they will have to pay much closer attention to what the Word says about them.

> **Are they [angels] not all ministering spirits, sent forth to minister for them who shall be heirs of salvation? Therefore we ought to give the more earnest heed to the things which we have heard, lest at any time we should let them slip. For if the word spoken by angels was stedfast, and every transgression and disobedience received a just recompence of reward; how shall we escape, if we neglect so great salvation; which at the first began to be spoken by the Lord.**
>
> **Hebrews 1:14-2:3**

Look again at verse 1, which says, **Therefore we ought to give the more earnest heed to the things which we have heard, lest at any time we should let them slip.** In the place of **earnest heed,** *The Amplified Bible* uses the phrase, **pay much closer attention than ever to.** In other words, the writer of Hebrews is giving us a stern warning telling us that angels are being sent to us as ministering servants. Therefore, we need to pay much closer attention to what the Word of God says about their ministry, lest at any time we should fail to take proper advantage of their services to us.

Another thing this particular passage teaches us about angels is that their word is **stedfast, and every transgression and disobedience receive[s] a just recompence of reward** (v. 2). What does that mean? It simply means that angels are sent forth by God, and they can't change the orders or words they have been given. When an angel speaks, it is stedfast. He can't alter what he says. He doesn't have the ability to forgive or extend mercy if you ignore his message. That isn't his job. Only God can do that.

THEIR WORD IS STEDFAST
...

Throughout the Bible, angels are seen doing two things: either ministering the blessing of God or administering the judgment of God. Sometimes they do both on the same trip. For example, the angel Gabriel appeared to Zacharias to bring a blessing and announce the glorious news that Zacharias' wife, who had been barren, was going to have a baby and that the baby's name was to be John. (Luke 1:5-25.)

But the Word makes it clear that Zacharias was in unbelief. Essentially, he responded to the angel by saying, "Give me a sign that I may know what you say is true." (Luke 1:18.) Sure enough, Gabriel gave him a sign. He told Zacharias that because of his unbelief, he would remain dumb until the baby was born. The word of Gabriel was steadfast, and Zacharias didn't speak until John was born. Gabriel made sure that Zacharias' tendency to speak words of doubt didn't thwart the plan of God.

We see the same truth demonstrated when the angels brought Lot and his family out of the doomed cities of Sodom and Gomorrah in Genesis 19:1-26. Two angels had been sent to deliver Lot and his family from the judgment that was about to fall. They were essentially on a rescue mission.

As they were leaving the city, one of the angels turned to Lot and said, "Don't look back!" Now, that word was intended to be a blessing to Lot and his family because terrible destruction was about to rain down on the cities they considered to be their home.

Many of the people they knew were about to experience the judgment of God, and there would be a tremendous amount of agony and suffering. The angel was trying to assure Lot and his family that the judgment wasn't intended for them. But Lot's wife looked back on the cities and turned into a pillar of salt. What the angel spoke was intended to be a blessing, but it became a judgment to Lot's wife because of her inappropriate response.

You see, angels are sent to minister to us, the heirs of salvation, but they can't extend mercy or grace. They are on assignment to minister blessing. They are sent to deliver us from the judgment that is already on the earth because of sin. And if we don't properly respond to them, we will miss the blessing and experience judgment instead, just as Lot's wife did.

DON'T NEGLECT SUCH A GREAT SALVATION
...

Unfortunately, the same tragedy can happen to us. That is precisely why Hebrews 2:3 warns us that we won't escape judgment either if we neglect so great a salvation.

For centuries, Christians have read that verse this way: "How shall we escape hell and damnation, if we neglect so great a salvation through Jesus?" And although that is certainly true, because we will escape hell and damnation through the salvation available to us through Jesus, that isn't what this verse is saying. If we interpret it in its context, we can see that the writer of Hebrews is still talking about the ministry of angels here. That is why Hebrews 2:1 begins with the word **therefore: Therefore we ought to give the more earnest heed to the things which we have heard.** What things? The things about angels and ministering spirits discussed in the previous verses! Why should we pay attention to those things? So that we won't miss out on the great salvation available to us through the ministry of angels.

That is what verse 3 is talking about here. It is saying, in essence, "How shall we escape the judgment or curse that is in the earth? How shall we escape impossible circumstances if we neglect so great a deliverance as the one available to us through angels?" This is the context in which salvation is being discussed. It is in the context of angelic ministry.

Verse 3 of this same passage goes on to say, **which at the first began to be spoken by the Lord.** It refers to the fact that Jesus spoke about angels at the beginning of His ministry.

Look at John 1:51, and you can see that for yourself. Jesus said, **Verily, verily, I say unto you, Hereafter ye shall see heaven open, and the angels of God ascending and descending upon the Son of man.** What picture does that paint for you? It depicts angels going up and coming down—heavenly beings going back and forth ministering to the heirs of salvation!

Later in His ministry, Jesus referred again to the service of angels. He was in the Garden of Gethsemane with His disciples. A great multitude of people, led by the chief priests and elders, had entered the garden in order to seize Jesus and take Him to Caiaphas to stand trial. As the mob surrounded Jesus, Peter drew his sword and cut off the ear of one of the servants of the chief priests. Jesus stopped Peter and proceeded to heal the man's ear.

Then Jesus said, **Thinkest thou that I cannot now pray to my Father, and he shall presently give me more than twelve legions of angels?** (Matthew 26:53). There were 6,000 men in a Roman legion, and Jesus said He could call up twelve legions of angels if He needed them. That is 72,000 angels! Later in this book, you will see that *one* angel is capable of more than we can imagine, so just think what 72,000 angels are capable of doing! And Jesus said He could call them up instantly if He so needed.

In light of that, think again about what I've been saying. Jesus is the firstborn of many brethren, and we are His heirs. (Romans 8:29.) If He can summon twelve legions of angels to come to His aid, guess who else can call upon twelve legions of angels? That's right. We can!

This is the great salvation the writer of Hebrews is talking about. This is the great source of deliverance spoken about by Jesus throughout His ministry. It is confirmed later by the apostles and other New Testament writers. The ministry of angels is real, and it is vital to our lives here on this earth. It is part of God's supernatural provision for you as a Christian. But remember, if you neglect this great source of deliverance, you won't escape the difficult places you will encounter in this life.

So pay close attention and give earnest heed to this ministry and to what the Word says about it. You certainly don't want to miss out on this great salvation!

C H A P T E R   5

Messengers of Mercy
•••

One very encouraging fact has become clear to me as I've studied what the Bible has to say about angels. *God doesn't send them because we deserve them. He sends them because we need help.* Angels are literally messengers of God's mercy. Think again about Lot and his family, and you will see what I mean. Angels brought deliverance to them from the impending judgment and destruction of Sodom and Gomorrah, even though they had of their own free will chosen to live in those evil cities. (Genesis 19:1-26.) Lot didn't really deserve the personal angelic escort that took him to safety, yet God sent one anyway.

IN YOUR MOMENT OF NEED
•••

We see a similar example in the account of Elijah given in 1 Kings, chapters 18 and 19. There, we find that Elijah had just experienced the power of God in a mighty way. God had poured out fire from heaven in answer to his prayers and enabled him to defeat four hundred idolatrous prophets of Baal.

This, however, infuriated Queen Jezebel, so she threatened to kill Elijah. When he heard of it, Elijah was so terrified that he ran for his life and hid in the wilderness, where he quickly sank into a pit of depression, doubt and despair. The Bible says:

> And he requested for himself that he might die; and said, It is enough; now, O Lord, take away my life; for I am not better than my fathers. And as he lay and slept under a juniper tree, behold, then an angel touched him, and said unto him, Arise and eat.
>
> And he looked, and, behold, there was a cake baken on the coals, and a cruse of water at his head. And he did eat and drink, and laid him down again. And the angel of the Lord came again the second time, and touched him, and said, Arise and eat; because the journey is too great for thee. And he arose, and did eat and drink, and went in the strength of that meat forty days and forty nights unto Horeb the mount of God.
>
> 1 Kings 19:4-8

Think of it! Elijah had run away in doubt and fear on the heels of one of God's greatest displays of power. Certainly, at that moment, Elijah didn't deserve God's mercy. Nevertheless, God sent an angel, a messenger of mercy, to sustain him and encourage him.

Another interesting point to notice is that in this account, as in almost every other account in both the Old and New Testaments, the visitation of an angel came immediately at the moment of greatest need. It came right on time! God didn't wait around for the person in need to prove himself deserving of intervention; God moved *quickly*. Surely, He is rich in mercy and delights in demonstrating His love and compassion!

That is wonderful news for every Christian. Why? Because we *all* need the mercy of God. All of us make mistakes from time to time and need immediate help. And through the ministry of angels, that help can come to us right on time.

ANGELS IN THE COCKPIT
...

One such incident happened to a man I'll call Henry. He was a pilot. And since I'm a pilot, I have been particularly fascinated by his story, which was recently published in a secular magazine. His story goes something like this:

Henry is a private pilot, and a few years ago he was able to acquire a small, single-engine airplane of his own. The small plane could seat four people, and it was perfect for Henry. It enabled him to fly more, which he loved to do, and log the hours necessary to keep his license current. Soon after Henry got his plane, he learned that one of his friends had a family member who was battling cancer. The family member lived in another city, and Henry's friend had to make a number of trips to that city to visit the ailing relative. Henry saw this as an opportunity to help his friend and increase his hours in the air, so he offered to fly his friend once or twice a week to the city where the relative lived.

On one particular day in which he was going to make the trip, Henry ended up behind schedule. He was late to the airport, so he rushed through his preflight preparations. In his haste, he decided not to have the airplane refueled. After all, they were only flying a short distance—from Greenville to Ashville. They had more than enough fuel to make it. The weather forecast for that day was not great, but it wasn't too bad, either, he told himself.

Unfortunately, however, once they were airborne, the weather became worse than what had been forecast. As a result, Henry had to make several changes in his flight plan as air traffic control steered them around storms. By the time they reached Ashville, Henry's fuel gauge was bouncing on empty. They were barely going to make it. As Henry prepared for landing, the voice of the tower crackled over the radio, "The Ashville field is closed due to fog. You need to return to Greenville or go to your alternate location."

A wave of dismay swept over Henry as he realized the extent of the mistake he had made. "I don't have enough fuel to do either," he said to the operator. "I have to land now!"

"All right, then," answered the operator, "you are cleared for an ILS approach at zero-zero." Henry had been given permission to make an instruments-only landing in near-zero visibility.

Now there was just one problem. With the fog increasing, Henry was uncertain of his location. He had become distracted. He had lost his bearings and wasn't set up correctly for an ILS approach. Even so, he knew he had to start down on a blind descent. He was certain he would miss the airport and run out of fuel if he didn't.

About forty-five seconds into his descent, a new voice suddenly came rasping over the headset, "Pull up! Pull up!"

Quickly, Henry pulled up. As he did, he broke through the thick clouds and caught a glimpse of the ground. Not only had he missed the airport, but he was very low and over an interstate highway. There was a bridge directly in front of him. If he hadn't pulled up as commanded, he would have surely plowed into it.

As Henry drew a sharp breath, the new controller's voice came through the headset once again, "Follow my instructions, and we'll get you on the ground."

Gratefully, Henry responded. "Yes, thank you, and be aware that we are very short on fuel. We need to land very quickly."

The controller gave Henry the headings he needed to bring him back around again. He established Henry on a final approach and told him when to begin his descent. Then he gave Henry some course corrections coming down on final approach. They were exactly right. As the plane touched down, Henry caught a glimpse through the fog of the runway lights flashing by. He was squarely on the runway center line.

After Henry had landed and begun to taxi in to the terminal, he called the tower controller to thank him for his help, "I just want you to know that you saved our lives today!"

The tower controller sounded puzzled, "Say again?"

"I want to thank you," Henry repeated. "What you did today saved our lives."

"Sir, I lost contact with you when I told you the airport was closed," said the controller. "This is the first time I've talked with you since then."

After an hour or so on the telephone, it was verified that none of the approach controllers in the Ashville area had any kind of communication with Henry. When his story appeared in the magazine, it was entitled, "Angels in the Cockpit."[1]

LIVE BY FAITH
...

So often we get ourselves into situations where supernatural intervention is required. Usually, the reason we find ourselves in those situations is that, like Henry, we did something thoughtless or made a mistake. Aren't you glad we serve a God of mercy? I certainly am! **It is of the Lord's mercies that we are not consumed, because his compassions fail not. They are new every morning: great is thy faithfulness** (Lamentations 3:22,23).

Even though angel's assistance is a wonderful blessing, we aren't to live continually by the ministry of angels. The Bible says that the just shall live by *faith*. (Hebrews 10:38.) That is God's highest way for us. We are what we believe. And what we believe needs to be cultivated along the lines of God's Word. **For as he** [a man] **thinketh in his heart, so is he,** says Proverbs 23:7. And according to Mark 9:23, **If thou canst believe, all things are possible to him that believeth.**

"But, Mac," you might be thinking, "if we are called to live by faith and faith brings the answer, why do we even need the ministry of angels?" Well, that is a good question. And the answer is that we need their ministry because learning to live by faith is a process. It isn't something you decide to do today and then become an expert at tomorrow.

Faith begins with a decision, but it develops through spiritual growth. Romans 10:17 tells us, **Faith cometh by hearing, and hearing by the word of God.** The Word has to be planted in you. It has to be watered. It has to be cultivated. Through that process, faith comes. That is why Galatians 6:9 says, **Let us not be weary in well doing: for in due season we shall reap, if we faint not.** If we will keep on confessing the Word, meditating on the Word and acting on the Word, we will most certainly reap a harvest. When? In due season!

Sometimes, though, you will come up against a hard place in your life before your due season has arrived. You will encounter an emergency that you haven't yet developed the faith to handle. That is when you need God's immediate intervention. That is when you need a messenger of mercy to be involved in your circumstances. That is when you need a source of deliverance and provision other than your faith.

The ministry of angels has been given to us for just such times. They come as God's ministering spirits, sent forth on our behalf to enable us to escape those especially hard places in life.

Just as angels came to help Lot and his family, just as Elijah experienced the provision of God's mercy at the hand of a ministering spirit and just as the pilot was delivered from a fatal crash—that is the same kind of assistance that we can also expect as God's children. It is one of the ways God helps us while we are here on this earth, particularly as our faith deepens in Him. Thank God for His ministering spirits—angels!

Positioning Yourself for Angelic Assistance
•••

Many times God's messengers of mercy show up at our greatest point of need. Yet it is obvious that angels don't always intervene. There are times when they are desperately needed, but they don't assist.

For example, the people of Israel were taken into captivity many times in their history, whether by the Babylonians or Egyptians or others, and often there was no angelic rescue team to come to their aid. In other instances, however, God *did* intervene; mercy was extended or deliverance came at a crucial moment.

What made the difference? As I studied the various angelic visitations in the Bible with this question in mind, I noticed a pattern. I found there was a lifestyle—an attitude or an approach to living—that was common among individuals who received angelic help. In short, I noticed they met certain qualifications.

This is an encouraging discovery. Why? Because it tells us there is a way we, too, can live—an attitude and an approach to life we can embrace—that will enable God to dispatch angelic messengers of mercy for us just as He did for people in the Bible.

When you are in the middle of a hard season or when you have blown it, there is an answer. If you live a certain way and do certain things, the ministry of angels can be brought to bear in your life to help you when you need it most.

Please understand, I'm not suggesting there is some kind of magic formula that releases the power of angels. I'm simply pointing you toward a lifestyle that is clearly identified in the Word of God, a lifestyle that puts you in a position to operate in true spiritual power. You see, the way you live your life will have a direct impact on your ability to avail yourself of God's delivering power on a daily basis.

When Only God Can Help
• • •

Let's begin our investigation into the qualifications for angelic ministry by looking in Isaiah 36 and 37. There you will find the example of a man who clearly met those qualifications. It is an amazing story. It is the story of how Judah's king, Hezekiah, overcame the evil Sennacherib, king of Assyria, and the Assyrian army. It is also an example of the power of God's angels.

Isaiah 36 begins during the fourteenth year of King Hezekiah's reign. Sennacherib, king of Assyria, had come up against the cities of Judah and conquered them. He then set his sights on Jerusalem with plans to take it by siege. Sennacherib sent Rabshakeh to Jerusalem to meet with King Hezekiah. (Rabshakeh, as used here, isn't a man's name. It is a military term that refers to an office of state much like that of a modern-day Secretary of State. It literally means the king's representative charged with negotiating truces and surrenders.[1])

Sennacherib assumed that because of the destructive force of his great army, Hezekiah would surely surrender Jerusalem to him without a struggle. Therefore, Rabshakeh was sent to deliver the terms of surrender to Hezekiah. As Rabshakeh met with Hezekiah's representatives, he spoke so that all of the people of Jerusalem could hear. He warned them not to be persuaded by Hezekiah to trust in the Lord for deliverance. He reminded the people that the Assyrian army had just defeated the forces in Judah and that, frankly, nothing could stand in the way of King Sennacherib.

In order to get the full picture, let's back up a little and look at what had happened just prior to Rabshakeh's visit. Historically, this event took place in 701 B.C., and Assyria was the dominant power of that time. Assyrians had embarked on a two-year campaign to conquer the rest of the civilized world, and the primary obstacle standing in their way was Egypt. But in order to conquer Egypt, Assyria had to march south through Israel.[2]

Hezekiah had learned of the Assyrians' plans well in advance of their attack on the cities of Judah. He realized he didn't have the military strength to face the Assyrian army alone. So in an attempt to save his kingdom, Hezekiah had made an alliance with Egypt in direct disobedience to repeated instructions from the Lord.

Egypt was eager to make this alliance because if Judah turned the Assyrians back, the Egyptians would never have to fight them on their own soil. Thus, a pact was made. Egypt supplied Hezekiah with paid mercenaries to bolster his forces, and it was these combined forces that the Assyrian army had defeated at Lachish, one of the cities in Judah. In fact, this is the city from which Rabshakeh had come when he ordered the surrender of Jerusalem in Isaiah 36:2.

As he called for the surrender, he reminded the people of Israel that no alliance or nation had been able to stand up against the great Assyrian army. (Isaiah 36:5-7.) As Hezekiah listened to Rabshakeh's message, he realized he could no longer depend on natural, military might. His alliance with Egypt had failed him. Disaster was at the door, and only God could help him now.

REPENT, SEEK GOD'S WORD AND PRAY!
. . .

What did Hezekiah do to secure that divine help? Isaiah 37:1 tells us: **And it came to pass, when king Hezekiah heard it, that he rent his clothes, and covered himself with sackcloth, and went into the house of the Lord.** In other words, Hezekiah repented of his sin. What sin? The sin he had committed when he made the alliance with Egypt. For generations, it had been a standing order of the Lord not to enter into a covenant or an agreement with Egypt.

The second thing Hezekiah did was turn to the word of the Lord. According to Isaiah 37:2, **he sent Eliakim, who was over the household, and Shebna the scribe, and the elders of the priests covered with sackcloth, unto Isaiah the prophet the son of Amoz.** Hezekiah sought the word of the Lord as represented at that time by the prophet Isaiah.

The third thing Hezekiah did was pray. Look at what Isaiah 37:14 says, **And Hezekiah received the letter from the hand of the messengers, and read it: and Hezekiah went up unto the house of the Lord, and spread it before the Lord.** Earnestly, Hezekiah made his case before God in prayer saying:

44

> Incline thine ear, O Lord, and hear; open thine eyes, O Lord, and see: and hear all the words of Sennacherib, which hath sent to reproach the living God.... Now therefore, O Lord our God, save us from his hand, that all the kingdoms of the earth may know that thou art the Lord, even thou only.
>
> Isaiah 37:17,20

It is important to understand that Hezekiah couldn't have prayed that prayer if he hadn't first repented. Prayer isn't going to work if you are still walking on the wrong path and your heart is wrong. You first have to change and get in line with God. And that is exactly what Hezekiah did.

FOLLOW HEZEKIAH'S EXAMPLE
• • •

Do you know what happened in that situation? The Lord sent an angel to help Hezekiah. Verse 36 says, **The angel of the Lord went forth, and smote in the camp of the Assyrians a hundred and fourscore and five thousand: and when they arose early in the morning, behold, they were all dead corpses.** Hezekiah woke up the following morning and found out his enemies were all dead! God had sent His angel, who slew 185,000 soldiers of the most powerful army on the earth at that time—and he did it in one night. Friend, that is the way to fight a battle!

Thank heavens that Hezekiah qualified for that kind of assistance! He lived in such a way that he allowed God to send an angel on his behalf, even when he had blown it. Hezekiah was quick to repent. He sought out the Word of the Lord. And most importantly, he prayed.

That is the lesson for us today. We need to recognize those times when we fail or aren't in faith, and then we need to repent. Of course, true repentance calls for a change of direction.

Once you have repented, get in the Word. Study and meditate on God's promises. See what He says about your condition or circumstance. Finally, pray! Prayer is hard work, but don't give up. Press in and seek the Lord's face with an attitude of humility. Remember, this is a process, and this process is a way of living. It is an attitude we have and a lifestyle we embrace.

When we are quick to repent and determined to change our course, when we consistently spend time in God's Word and in prayer—*then* we are candidates for the ministry of angels. We open the way for God to send them to intervene on our behalf.

More Than a Safety Net
•••

As marvelous as God's merciful interventions are, the truth is that God intended the ministry of angels to be something more than a mere "safety net" for us when we begin sinking in our circumstances. Look at Exodus 23:20, and you will see what I mean.

God told the Israelites, **Behold, I send an Angel before thee, to keep thee in the way, and to bring thee into the place which I have prepared.** What He once did, He still does. That means He has assigned angels to go before you as His New Covenant child just as surely as He assigned them to go before His Old Covenant servants. Hebrews 13:8 tells us that Jesus Christ is the same yesterday, today and forever.

HIS ANGELS GO BEFORE YOU
•••

What does it mean for God to send angels before you? It means He dispatches them to make the way clear for you. He doesn't want your life to be characterized by crises and catastrophes. He sends angels before you to keep you on a safe path and to bring you into the destiny He has prepared for you. That is God's will for you!

Because angelic ministry is deployed to help you at all times, you don't have to live life bouncing from one emergency to the next. As Psalm 34:7 says, **The angel of the LORD *encampeth* round about them that fear him, and delivereth them.** In every area of life—in business and ministry, in finances and family affairs—God has commissioned angels to go before you to prepare the way. God's best is for us to understand enough about this angelic ministry to deliberately and consciously commission our angelic hosts on a daily basis. He would prefer that we avail ourselves of them in advance so they can help us avoid the hard places instead of simply waiting for them to rescue us when we get into trouble.

Allow me to clarify something at this point. When I say we "commission" the angels, I'm not saying we simply order our angels around. I believe God has made the ministry of angels available to us as a resource to enable us to fulfill our created destinies. But that doesn't mean we have them at our beck and call. We can't arrogantly order them about as we see fit. The angels wouldn't listen to our dumb ideas anyway because they get their instructions from God. They do *His* bidding on *our* behalf.

FOCUS ON THE UNSEEN
· · ·

With that said, let's examine how this angelic system works and find out what we can do to take better advantage of it in our daily lives. Let's start by looking at Hebrews 2:1 again, keeping in mind that it is referring to angelic ministry: **Therefore we ought to give the more earnest heed to the *things* which we have heard, lest at any time we should let them slip.** In Scripture, the word *things* is frequently used when making a distinction between the material realm and the spiritual realm. Look, for example, at the way Paul uses the word *things* in Colossians 3:2: **Set your affection on *things* above, not on *things* on the earth.**

If the ministry of angels is going to become a daily fact in our lives, there are some spiritual *things* to which we must give more earnest heed. We need to pay attention to the differences between the natural world and the world of the spirit. The Bible makes a clear distinction between these two realms. Consider Second Corinthians 4:17-18, which says,

> **For our light affliction, which is but for a moment, worketh for us a far more exceeding and eternal weight of glory; while we look not at the things which are seen, but at the things which are not seen: for the things which are seen are temporal; but the things which are not seen are eternal.**

Those verses are telling us that if we want our affliction or hardship to be light and momentary as opposed to something long and drawn out, then we must look not at the things which are seen, but at the things which are *not* seen. We need to look in the spiritual realm and not in the natural realm.

Obviously, we can't literally acquire visual acuity into the unseen, spiritual realm (unless God supernaturally gifts us to operate in the discerning of spirits and enables us to see with your natural eye into that realm). That isn't what this passage is saying. It is simply saying that the unseen realm needs to be the focus of our attention. It is telling us to give earnest heed to the unseen realm because it supersedes the temporal world in which we live. It is urging us to pay more attention to the spiritual realm than we do to what we can see, hear, touch, taste or smell.

Why? Because that is the realm in which you access the ministry of angels—angels who can get you through those hard places quickly and easily! But let me warn you. It won't be easy to give priority to the world of the Spirit rather than the temporal realm. It goes totally counter to everything your flesh wants to do.

You have spent years being conditioned to rely upon what you physically see, hear, taste, smell and feel. You have learned to rely upon your rational abilities when making decisions. It takes a major adjustment to begin basing your life and your decision-making processes on the unseen realm. But the fact of the matter is, if you don't make that adjustment, your afflictions won't be light. They will be long and hard. So it is worth the effort it takes to shift your focus from the realm of the natural to the realm of the Spirit.

GET GOD'S PERSPECTIVE
• • •

When you continually walk with God, it is actually possible for the unseen realm to become more real to you than what you see or hear in this natural world. I know this because the Bible tells us about people who lived that way. One of them was the prophet Elisha. In 2 Kings 6:8-10, the Bible gives us a glimpse of how he operated in regard to the unseen realm. It tells us that during Elisha's ministry,

> The king of Syria warred against Israel, and took counsel with his servants, saying, In such and such a place shall be my camp. And [Elisha] the man of God sent unto the king of Israel, saying, Beware that thou pass not such a place; for thither the Syrians are come down. And the king of Israel sent to the place which the man of God told him

and warned him of, and saved himself there, not once nor twice.

Do you get the picture here? Elisha is spoiling every battle plan the Syrian king can devise. By the word of knowledge, he finds out what the plans of the enemy are and tells the king of Israel about them in advance. As a result, the Syrians are left looking like fools! The passage goes on to say,

> Therefore the heart of the king of Syria was sore troubled for this thing; and he called his servants, and said unto them, Will ye not shew me which of us is for the king of Israel? And one of his servants said, None, my lord, O king: but Elisha, the prophet that is in Israel, telleth the king of Israel the words that thou speakest in thy bedchamber.
>
> And he said, Go and spy where he is, that I may send and fetch him. And it was told him, saying, Behold, he is in Dothan. Therefore sent he thither horses, and chariots, and a great host: and they came by night, and compassed the city about. And when the servant of the man of God was risen early, and gone forth, behold, an host compassed the city both with horses and chariots. And his servant said unto him, Alas, my master! how shall we do?
>
> 2 Kings 6:11-15

Actually, a more contemporary paraphrase of the Hebrew exclamation made by Elisha's servants would be, "We've had it, master! We're dead meat!" But Elisha remained calm and answered his servant, saying,

> Fear not: for they that be with us are more than they that be with them. And Elisha prayed, and said, Lord, I pray thee, open his eyes, that he may see. And the Lord opened the eyes of the young man; and he saw: and, behold, the moun-

tain was full of horses and chariots of fire round about Elisha.

2 Kings 6:16,17

Friend, let me ask you a question. If God would send this kind of angelic help for Elisha, won't He do it for you? The Bible says God is no respecter of persons. (Romans 2:11.) We know that angels are on assignment to serve our needs. Elisha needed an army, so God provided one. Wouldn't He do the same for you? Certainly, He would! In fact, He already has. He has commissioned untold thousands of angels to minister on behalf of all of us who are heirs of salvation. Why haven't we benefited from them as fully as Elisha did? Because we haven't had his perspective!

Think again about how Elisha responded to his situation. When his servant came to him in great fear, Elisha could have seen with his natural eye the grave circumstances. He could have been terrified as his young servant was, but he wasn't. As a prophet of God, Elisha didn't rely strictly on what he could see and hear. He had developed a sense for what was happening in the spirit realm, and he put far more confidence in that realm than he did in the natural realm!

We can learn to be the same way. We can develop our spiritual eyes and ears by spending more time focusing on the spiritual realm. As we spend more time in the Word and in prayer, we can learn to shift our attention away from temporal things and onto eternal realities. Remember, this is a process, and it takes time. But you can take the first step in that process by making a decision today to focus on the unseen realm.

CHAPTER 8

The Prayer Connection
• • •

The unseen realm of the spirit has much more going on in it than most people ever realize and is teeming with powerful activity. Even so, Christians fail to give it much thought.

Why is that? Primarily because the seen realm—the natural realm—constantly clamors for our attention. Our natural senses are continually assaulted with stimuli from that realm. It is no wonder that the spiritual realm is so often neglected. The noise of the natural realm drowns it out!

The good news is, we *can* make a conscious decision to tune out the clamor of the natural realm—what we see, hear, touch, taste and smell—and tune into the supernatural realm as revealed to us through the Word of God. We can train ourselves to be more responsive to the unseen realm than we are to that which is seen.

Actually, everyone responds to the spiritual realm in one way or another, whether they realize it or not. In this chapter, I want to examine four kinds of typical responses to spiritual things as seen in the account from 2 Kings 6:8-17, which we looked at in the previous chapter, and briefly consider an example of each because we see the same responses today.

SPIRITUAL REALM? WHAT SPIRITUAL REALM?
• • •

The first type of response I want you to notice is that of the king of Syria. His response is basically that of denial. He acts as if the spiritual realm doesn't exist. When he has a problem, he doesn't even consider the possibility that the unseen realm may be the root of his problem. He simply assumes a natural explanation. He assumes that Israel has learned about his battle plans because someone in his camp is a spy.

Because he denies the existence of the spiritual realm, he immediately turns to a natural solution. He lashes out in anger at those closest to him and accuses them. In his mind, they are the only natural and obvious reason for the failure of his battle plans.

I see that pattern repeated again and again in people today. Because they don't understand that their problem originates outside the natural realm, they don't even look to the unseen realm to see how their problem might be solved. Instead, they respond by getting frustrated and angry. They usually lash out at those around them, especially the people who are closest to them. For these natural-minded people, there is no other explanation for the difficulty they are facing. Therefore, they respond this way over and over again.

The second response is similar to the first, and we see an example of it in Elisha's servant. He was similar to the Syrian king in that he didn't give the unseen realm credit for the problem. But the servant's reaction was different. Unlike the king who lashed out in anger, the servant allowed fear to rise up in him. He wanted to flee the situation. He saw the great Syrian army and realized there was no *natural* hope for his survival or for the survival of his master, Elisha.

"LET'S GO GET HIM, GUYS!"
• • •

The third example of a person's reaction to the unseen realm can be seen in the king of Syria *after* he learned that something was indeed happening in an unseen realm. His servant was able to convince him that his problem wasn't a natural one but rather that God was showing a prophet in Israel the king's plans. When the king began to understand that his problem was supernatural, he became aware of another realm of reality. When he sent out his army to capture Elisha, he acknowledged the possibility of the spiritual realm.

Personally, however, it strikes me as funny that the king of Syria thought he could catch Elisha. He had already been told that Elisha could hear what he was saying in his bedroom. What made him think he could sneak up on Elisha now? Didn't it occur to the king that Elisha could hear the plans he was making for his capture?

Be that as it may, the king did finally acknowledge the unseen realm. But he responded to his spiritual problem by applying a natural solution. He said to his soldiers, "If Elisha can hear in the spirit, then let's go get *him*!" This is the mistake many Christians make today. For years, they have been taught about the two different realms, and most would affirm their belief in those two realms. They know that the Bible says we war not against flesh and blood, but against principalities, powers, rulers of darkness and spiritual wickedness in high places. (Ephesians 6:12.)

There is more to life than what meets the eye, and most Christians realize this. They see that the real challenges in their lives come from the unseen realm. But like the king of Syria, they are still trying to meet those challenges by applying strictly natural solutions. If they run out of money, they say, "Let's go get another loan at the bank." If they get sick, they say, "Let's go to a doctor and get some help." If they run into trouble, they say, "Let's figure this out rationally."

Let me assure you, I don't have any problem with people who borrow money from the bank or go to doctors and use medicine. None of these practices are wrong in themselves. In fact, they all have a place in our lives as we grow in God. However, I *don't* believe they are God's best way for us.

DON'T PANIC—PRAY
...

The fourth response, Elisha's, is obviously the correct response to a spiritual problem. Consider the way he dealt with this potentially life-threatening situation. He relied totally on the resources and power of the unseen realm. He based his decision-making process upon what was happening in the spiritual realm instead of what was happening in the natural realm. And this time, Elisha wanted his servant to have the benefit of understanding that higher realm, so he said, **Lord, I pray thee, open his eyes, that he may see** (2 Kings 6:17).

Now this is what I want you to notice. When it was necessary for the servant to see that which was unseen—for him to give earnest heed and pay close attention to the realm of the unseen—Elisha prayed. It was prayer that opened up the servant's awareness and enabled him to see into that realm. The servant panicked, but Elisha prayed!

Prayer has been involved in every example of angelic intervention we have seen so far. Prayer is what opens you to the reality of the unseen realm. If you aren't a person who prays, you will never experience the reality of the spirit realm. And by prayer, I don't mean those token, three-minute religious tidbits you throw out to appease your conscience. That isn't the kind of prayer I'm talking about here. Real prayer involves a relationship with God. It is communion with Him. It is communicating with Him on a regular basis.

Prayer has to be a part of your life if the unseen realm is going to become real to you. It is the only thing that brings that realm into sufficient focus. Time and again in this study you are going to see this. You can't appropriate the ministry of angels without having a vital, dynamic prayer life. The unseen realm in which angels operate will make no sense to you. It will forever elude you until you begin giving your life over to prayer.

SOME PRAYERS WORK, OTHERS DON'T
• • •

Prayer is the key, but not just any prayer will do. Some kinds of prayers don't work. James 4:2,3 tells us why:

> **Ye lust, and have not: ye kill, and desire to have, and cannot obtain: ye fight and war, yet ye have not, because ye ask not. Ye ask, and receive not, because ye ask amiss, that ye may consume it upon your lusts.**

It is possible to pray and still fail to receive. It is very simple: You ask and receive not because you ask to consume it upon your lust. In other words, a prayer motivated by pure self-interest is a prayer that won't be answered. Sadly enough, many prayers fall into this category. Most people don't pray until they have a need so great they can't deal with it on their own. Something happens—some circumstance or situation overwhelms them. First they try to solve the problem in their own strength and fail. So now it is time to pray.

But what are they doing? They are praying a prayer motivated by desperate self-interest. And because God loves them and is full of mercy, He will sometimes answer those prayers. But that isn't the type of prayer that believers are promised God will consistently answer.

Jesus said, **Whatsoever ye shall ask in my name, that will I do** (John 14:13). But we must ask in line with the Word, and the Word says that a prayer rooted in selfishness won't be answered. God can't answer that prayer because we would only consume whatever He brought into our lives upon ourselves—upon our desires and our own agendas.

That is why the message of service to others is so important. That is why it is vital to be conscious of other people's needs. This is bottom-line Christianity. Your purpose in life isn't to meet your own needs. Your purpose is to be a tool in the hand of God to meet somebody else's need. When you do that, He can use someone to meet your need.

The Word of God says that you give first, and then it will be given unto you. (Luke 6:38.) Your resources of time, talent and money aren't to be squandered on your own agenda. They are to be used as a resource to meet someone else's need.

That is God's plan, plain and simple. It is His plan for all of us! And until we get this message, nothing about our Christianity is going to work as it should, including our prayer lives.

If you have any doubts about it, get out your Bible and read the book of Job. Do you remember what happened to Job? He moaned and groaned and cried to God about his circumstances for almost forty chapters. He even blamed God for his problems, and nothing happened. No deliverance came. No healing came. He remained mired in the same terrible situation.

It was only when Job began to pray for his friends and their need that he received the answer to his own prayers. When Job prayed for his friends, God delivered him and gave him twice as much as he had before.

Job's success in prayer came from getting his eyes off his own problems (and they were certainly terrible!) and focusing on the needs of someone else. That is what he had to do in order to receive what he needed from God.

The same principle applies today. When you get your eyes off your needs and begin concentrating on what you can do to address the need in somebody else's life, God can then move on your behalf. That doesn't mean that your needs won't get met. It means that God is now able to meet them instead of you trying to meet them. And it is a better deal when God meets our needs because His resources are limitless.

This is the key to the kind of prayer that opens you to the realm of the Spirit. It is the prayer that emanates from a heart free of self-interest. I call this "making the prayer connection."

We said in the last chapter that the first step in appropriating the ministry of angels is to begin shifting your focus from the natural realm to the realm of the spirit. Always remember that the way you do that is through prayer. As you pray from a pure heart, undefiled by self-interest, the realm of the spirit begins to take on a measure of reality. You establish a prayer connection in the unseen realm.

This is the first thing that has to happen before you can appropriate the angelic ministry available to you through that realm. It will come no other way. Until prayer has the priority it should in your life, the unseen realm won't be a reality to you.

Elisha understood this principle. He had given his life over to prayer. He had a prayer connection. Whenever he faced a perilous or difficult situation, he didn't rely upon that which he could see in the natural. He looked to God through prayer and was continuously delivered.

If you will give yourself over to prayer, you, too, will begin to see and experience the mighty deliverance of God!

Speak the Right Words
•••

After you become fully aware of the presence and activity of the unseen realm of the spirit, there is a second step in the process of appropriating the ministry of angels. It can be summarized in one short phrase: *speak the right words*.

It is impossible to overestimate the importance of our words because words generate the most powerful force there is—the force of faith. As Romans 10:17 says, **faith cometh by hearing, and hearing by the word of God.** Our words control our believing, our thinking, our behavior and even the direction our lives will take. James 3:3-5 puts it this way:

> **Behold, we put bits in the horses' mouths, that they may obey us; and we turn about their whole body. Behold also the ships, which though they be so great, and are driven of fierce winds, yet are they turned about with a very small helm, whithersoever the governor listeth. Even so the tongue is a little member, and boasteth great things.**

One of the greatest lies Satan has sold humanity can be summed up in the brief rhyme we all are familiar with: "Sticks and stones may break my bones, but words will never hurt me." In reality, the very opposite is true. Words will either make us or break us. Proverbs 18:21 says it this way: **Death and life are in the power of the tongue.**

Why are our words so crucial? One big reason is that the words we speak either bind or loose those ministering spirits mentioned in the first chapter of Hebrews. Jesus said that whatever we as believers bind on this earth is bound also in heaven and whatever we loose on this earth is also loosed in heaven. (Matthew 16:19.) Certainly this applies to the angelic host.

Psalm 103:20,21 gives us even further insight into how our words affect angelic activity. It says, **Bless the Lord, ye his angels, that excel in strength, that do his commandments, hearkening unto the voice of his word. Bless ye the Lord, all ye his hosts; ye ministers of his, that do his pleasure.**

Notice that these verses refer to angels as those who **excel in strength** (v. 20). They identify the supernatural capacity angels have to impact this physical world. We have seen scriptural evidence of that already. Do you remember what one angel did to the 185,000 Assyrians in Isaiah 37:36? He killed them all in a single night! Obviously, when you have angels at work for you, you have an absolutely awesome source of power at your disposal.

Psalm 103:21 further identifies angels as ministers of God **that do his pleasure.** It doesn't say they do His dirty work. God doesn't have any dirty work. It says they do His pleasure, and according to Psalm 35:27, God takes pleasure in the prosperity of His servant.

God doesn't take pleasure in your insufficiency or lack. He doesn't take pleasure in your sickness. He takes pleasure in blessing you. He takes pleasure in prospering you. And

His angels are the ones who help deliver those blessings into your life.

What releases the angels to make these wonderful deliveries? Once again, the answer is found in Psalm 103:20, where it says that the angels hearken to the voice of God's Word. The word *hearken* in the Hebrew text means "obey."[1] In other words, angels obey the voice of God's Word. They don't obey your voice or your panicky plea for help. They don't obey anything but the voice of His Word.

And let me add this. Angels don't respond to the Bible that just lies on your coffee table either. They don't respond to written pages in a book because the written Word, by itself, has no voice. So, you can't just lift up your Bible and expect the angels to take off and do whatever needs to be done.

If you want the angels to have something to work with, you have to put voice to the Word of God. Don't put voice to your fear and unbelief; they won't respond to that. Put voice to the Word of God in faith. When you hide the Word of God in your heart and then speak it out as a confession of faith, you put the angels in motion!

DELIVERED FROM THE FIRE
• • •

You can see this principle in operation in the book of Daniel. There you will find the familiar story of Shadrach, Meshach and Abednego, three praying men who loved and worshipped God.

Shadrach, Meshach and Abednego were Jewish captives in Babylon at the time when the wicked King Nebuchadnezzar made a decree that anyone who worshipped a god other than his god would suffer the consequences. Unmoved by the king's decree, the three devout Hebrews continued in their worship of the most high God. As a result, they were brought before Nebuchadnezzar for punishment, and he said to them:

> Is it true, O Shadrach, Meshach, and Abednego, do not ye serve my gods, nor worship the golden image which I have set up? Now if ye be ready that at what time ye hear the sound of the cornet, flute, harp, sackbut, psaltery, and dulcimer, and all kinds of musick, ye fall down and worship the image which I have made; well: but if ye worship not, ye shall be cast the same hour into the midst of a burning fiery furnace; and who is that God that shall deliver you out of my hands?
>
> Daniel 3:14,15

Now, I want you to pay careful attention to the way these three men responded to the king's ultimatum. Watch what they said:

> Shadrach, Meshach, and Abednego, answered and said to the king, O Nebuchadnezzar, we are not careful to answer thee in this matter. If it be so, our God whom we serve is able to deliver us from the burning fiery furnace, and he will deliver us out of thine hand, O king. But if not, be it known unto thee, O king, that we will not serve thy gods, nor worship the golden image which thou hast set up.
>
> Daniel 3:16-18

People constantly misinterpret that last verse. They read it this way, "If God doesn't deliver us—if it isn't the will of God to save us—then we still aren't going to worship the golden image." But that interpretation makes no sense. Obviously, if God didn't deliver them, they wouldn't be worshipping anybody. They would be consumed in the fire! So there must be another meaning.

Read the verse again in context, and you will see what it really means. Verse 17 begins, **If it be so.** Verse 18 begins, **But if not.** They are both talking about the same thing. What? Being thrown into the fiery furnace! Shadrach, Meshach and Abednego were saying, "King, if it be so that you throw us into the fiery furnace, our God is going to deliver us. But if not, if you don't throw us into the fiery furnace, we still aren't going to worship your god." Notice that these three men all had the same confession of their faith: "God is able to deliver, and He *will* deliver!"

When they refused to obey him, Nebuchadnezzar ordered that the furnace be heated up seven times hotter than normal. It was so hot that the men who threw Shadrach, Meshach and Abednego into the furnace were instantly burned alive. But what happened next came as a shock to Nebuchadnezzar because when he looked into the furnace, he saw not three men, but four!

Then he turned to his counselors in alarm and said, **Did not we cast three men bound into the midst of the fire?** And the counselors answered, **True, O king.** Then the king exclaimed, **Lo, I see four men loose, walking in the midst of the fire, and they have no hurt; and the form of the fourth is like the Son of God** (vv. 24,25).

I'm sure you know the rest of the story. Shadrach, Meshach and Abednego were called out of the furnace. The king and all of his counselors marveled over the fact that they were not only unharmed but that they didn't even smell like smoke! Nebuchadnezzar was so impressed that he said, **Blessed be the God of Shadrach, Meshach, and**

Abednego, who hath sent his angel, and delivered his servants that trusted in him (v. 28). The fourth man in the furnace, although he looked like the Son of God, was identified as an angel.

The point I want to make here is that Shadrach, Meshach and Abednego got into trouble because they were men who loved God. But they had a prayer connection to the unseen realm that brought them deliverance from that trouble. That is the first step.

Second, the three men put the Word of God in their mouth. They said, "Our God is not only able, but He *will* deliver us." Basically, they said the same thing God said in Psalm 34:7, **The angel of the Lord encampeth round about them that fear him, and delivereth them.** They spoke God's Word and, sure enough, an angel responded to it. He showed up there in the midst of that burning fiery furnace and brought out Shadrach, Meshach and Abednego safe and sound.

Shutting the Lions' Mouths
· · ·

Later in the book of Daniel, we see yet another example of angelic assistance, this time in the life of Daniel himself. Daniel was a committed man of God and a man of prayer who, like his three friends, ran into one of the king's ungodly decrees. There is one difference, however. This king, Darius, liked Daniel. He liked him so much that he had elevated him to the highest level of authority in the land even though, technically, Daniel was a captive.

When Darius passed an ordinance that prohibited all prayer except that which was offered to an idol he had erected, Daniel was forced to disobey the king. He continued his practice of praying three times a day to the God of Israel. And since the king had already commanded that anyone who violated the ordinance be thrown into the den of lions, that is exactly what was done to Daniel.

The king was greatly dismayed about the situation, but there was nothing he could do. He had backed himself into a corner with his own decree. So as they hauled Daniel away to the lions' den, the king spoke these words of help and hope to him: **Daniel, Thy God whom thou servest continually, he will deliver thee** (Daniel 6:16). Actually, without realizing it, King Darius was giving voice to a faith confession of the Word of God.

That night, the king had a restless night. The next morning he rose early to check on Daniel. But instead of finding a pile of bones in the lions' den, the king found Daniel alive and well, saying, **O king, live for ever. My God hath sent his angel, and hath shut the lions' mouths, that they have not hurt me** (vv. 21,22).

Here again we see angelic deliverance provided for a man who was committed to prayer, a man who had a prayer connection to the unseen realm. We also see someone (in this case, the king) giving voice to the Word of God so that an angel could be dispatched.

"I Have Come for Thy Words"
...

Then in Daniel 10, we find yet another example of angelic assistance. In this account, we read about Daniel and the various dreams and visions he received. At this time, he had been seeking God for the freedom of his people from captivity in Babylon.

It is in this context that we read in verse 2, **In those days I Daniel was mourning three full weeks.** The Hebrew interpretation of this verse is a little different than what is rendered in the *King James* translation because Daniel's mourning as used here wasn't over a death but over the captivity of God's people in Babylon. Possibly the Hebrew word translated *mourning* here would have been better translated *lamenting* because as Daniel interceded for his people, he felt the heaviness of their burden and was in deep sorrow.[2]

Because Daniel was looking to God for an answer, he went on a partial fast, denying himself anything pleasant in order not to be distracted. Verse 3 tells us that **he ate no pleasant bread, neither came flesh nor wine in my mouth, neither did I anoint myself at all, till three whole weeks were fulfilled.**

Some people might think such fasting is merely an Old Testament ritual, but it is more than that. It is a spiritual tool that Jesus Himself taught and utilized. Do you remember the incident recorded in Matthew 17 where Jesus' disciples tried but failed to cast a demon spirit out of a young boy? They asked Jesus why they were unable to do it, and He answered, **This kind goeth not out but by prayer and fasting** (Matthew 17:21).

This is a spiritual principle. There will be times when we will encounter different levels of resistance in the unseen realm. And if our prayers aren't producing the desired effect, we may need to turn up the intensity. One way to do that is by fasting. When a person fasts, it just means that he denies the flesh of something it wants in order to be more attentive to things in the spiritual realm.

Thus, we see Daniel's fasting along with his praying. As a result, he has a vision. In Daniel 10:5,6, he says:

> Then I lifted up mine eyes, and looked, and behold a certain man clothed in linen, whose loins were girded with fine gold of Uphaz: His body also was like the beryl, and his face as the appearance of lightning, and his eyes as lamps of fire, and his arms and his feet like in colour to polished brass, and the voice of his words like the voice of a multitude.

Along with the vision appeared an angel who was sent to interpret the vision. The angel spoke to Daniel saying, **O Daniel, a man greatly beloved, understand the words that I speak unto thee** (Daniel 10:11). The angel then told Daniel to stand up and not be afraid. Daniel was clearly overwhelmed at the presence of the angel, but he managed to stand, trembling.

The angel continued in verse 12, **Fear not, Daniel: for from the first day that thou didst set thine heart to understand, and to chasten thyself before thy God, thy words were heard, and I am come for thy words.** The Bible is very clear on this point. The angel came to Daniel for his words. Once again, we see an angel responding to the voice of God's Word coming from the mouth of a man.

Overcoming Spiritual Resistance
• • •

I also want you to notice what the angel told Daniel next:

> But the prince of the kingdom of Persia withstood me one and twenty days: but, lo, Michael, one of the chief princes, came to help me;

69

**and I remained there with the kings of Persia. Now
I am come to make thee understand what shall
befall thy people in the latter days: for yet the
vision is for many days.**

Daniel 10:13,14

The angel that came to assist Daniel had encountered
spiritual resistance of a magnitude and sort that we have
no ability to understand. Unless God supernaturally opens
the spirit realm to us, we can't begin to imagine what goes
on there. We do know by reading the Word of God,
however, that this realm is populated not only by God's
angelic hosts, but by evil, fallen angels as well. And the
unified purpose of those fallen angels is to resist the will and
plan of God.

When they ascertain that something is beginning to
happen in God's plan, the powers and principalities band
together. Their resistance gets tougher. In this case, one of
God's chief angels, Michael, had to be dispatched in order to
make the breakthrough. And it took three weeks to do it!

Thank heavens, Daniel didn't quit praying! If he had
given up around the second week and said, "Well, I've done
my best, but I still don't have an answer," the angel
wouldn't have been able to complete his mission. The angel
came because of Daniel's words. As long as the words were
being spoken, as long as *voice* was being given to God's
Word, as long as Daniel pressed in and continued to seek
God on the matter, the angel kept fighting his way through
to bring the answer.

Daniel received the help he needed because he
maintained his diligence. He fasted and denied his flesh in
order to heighten his sensitivity to the unseen realm. He was
serious about it. He was determined to hear from God. We

need to be the same way. The Bible says that God rewards those who diligently seek Him. (Hebrews 11:6.)

Because **we wrestle not against flesh and blood, but against principalities, against powers, against the rulers of the darkness of this world, against spiritual wickedness in high places** (Ephesians 6:12), there can be incredible spiritual resistance in the unseen realm—resistance we don't fully comprehend. But just because we don't often comprehend what is going on behind the scenes, that doesn't mean we should quit. On the contrary, our part is to be consistent in prayer and consistent in speaking the Word.

With our words, we either bind the angelic ministering spirits, or we loose them to do God's pleasure. Therefore, we need to obey the Word of God when it says, **Let us not be weary in well doing: for in due season we shall reap, if we faint not** (Galatians 6:9). We need to keep on praying and giving voice to the Word of God!

CHAPTER 10

Five Levels of Words

• • •

If we are ever going to experience the full benefit of the ministry of angels, we will need a complete understanding of the powerful, yet simple, relationship of our words to the angelic realm. I feel so strongly about the importance of this relationship that I want to spend one more chapter examining the impact it has on our lives.

First of all, I believe that all the words we speak can be divided into five basic levels or categories. These different levels of words span the range of extremes between life and death. We can speak words of pure life, words of pure death or words somewhere between the two. Proverbs 18:21 warns us, **Death and life are in the power of the tongue: and they that love it shall eat the fruit thereof.** In other words, whatever words you say with your mouth, whether they fall in the category of life or death, will determine the fruit your life produces.

This is a reality that escapes most people. Yet our words impact virtually every aspect of who we are and the quality of life we presently experience. As I have mentioned, those words range between life and death on five basic levels.

WORDS OF LIFE

• • •

The first level, or the highest level, are the words of life. Obviously, these are the words we want to speak because they produce the God-kind of life. These are the words that enable the ministering angels to bring us the blessings of God and the grace of God that will promote the experience of eternal life. These are the words to which the angels respond.

When sincerely spoken, words of life are accompanied by behavior that is consistent with them. It is behavior that could be described as acting on God's Word, or as James 1:22 says, **Be ye doers of the word.** Being a doer of the Word means that we not only speak the Word of God, but we also order our life by what it says. It means we have made a decision to base our actions on what we find in the Word of God.

When we have done that, we begin walking out the will of God for our lives. As we speak the Word, we loose the ministering spirits to do His pleasure, which is to prosper us in our way.

THE VOCABULARY OF SILENCE

• • •

Now let's look at the second level of words and the accompanying behavior. These words will still produce life, but not to the same degree as the words of life. I call this level of communication the vocabulary of silence.

The Bible teaches that if you can't put voice to God's Word, the next best thing to do is to say nothing at all. There are numerous examples of this in the Bible. Consider Zacharias, for instance. The angel Gabriel visited Zacharias to tell him of the birth of his son, John the Baptist. (Luke 1:5-20.) But it became apparent to Gabriel that Zacharias didn't believe. If the plan of God was to go forth, he realized that something would have to be done about Zacharias' mouth. So Gabriel said, **Behold, thou shalt be dumb, and not able to speak, until the day that these things shall be performed** (Luke 1:20).

Now, Zacharias loved God. He believed in God's Word. But he had to have his mouth shut so he couldn't say the wrong thing until after the will of God was manifested. That is an example of the vocabulary of silence at work.

We see the same principle in operation in the Old Testament when the Israelites fought the battle of Jericho. Joshua, the military commander of the group, was given instructions by the Lord on how to take the city, and they were wild instructions! He was told:

> **And ye shall compass the city, all ye men of war, and go round about the city once. Thus shalt thou do six days. And seven priests shall bear before the ark seven trumpets of ram's horns: and the seventh day ye shall compass the city seven times, and the priests shall blow with the trumpets.**
>
> **And it shall come to pass, that when they make a long blast with the ram's horn, and when ye hear the sound of the trumpet, all the people shall shout with a great shout; and the wall of the city shall fall down flat.**
>
> Joshua 6:3-5

This was the supernatural instruction for battle that Joshua received. He wasn't going to get through the fortified walls of Jericho any other way. But I want you to notice something Joshua did. This is very interesting to me. When

75

Joshua relayed the battle plans to the children of Israel, he added something. He commanded the people, saying,

> **Ye shall not shout, nor make any noise with your voice, neither shall any word proceed out of your mouth, until the day I bid you shout; then shall ye shout.**

> **Joshua 6:10**

God didn't say anything about the people having to be quiet during the six days when they were to march around the city, but Joshua did. Joshua knew his people well enough to predict what they might say. They were whiners! So Joshua commanded them to be quiet. He didn't want them to jeopardize the battle with their complaining and doubt-filled words. You can imagine what some of those people would have said if they hadn't been under strict orders to be quiet, especially the men of war!

The men were all dressed for battle, but there was no one to fight. "It's hot out here, and this armor is heavy! What do you think has gotten into Joshua? Has he gone crazy? When are we going to attack? Look at them up there on the walls. They're all laughing at us!"

Can't you just hear them talk? They would have been just like you and me. To me, however, the principle is clear: If you are at a place in your life where you might be moved by circumstances and you aren't really certain you can speak in faith, then keep your mouth *shut* because there is ample scriptural precedent for not saying anything at all.

It isn't the highest way, but the vocabulary of silence will get you through when you are struggling in your faith. If you will just keep quiet as you continue to do the Word and to put it in your heart, your faith will grow. Before long, you will move up to the highest level and start speaking words of life.

WATCH OUT FOR IDLE WORDS
• • •

In Matthew 12:36, we read about the third level of words. There Jesus said, **Every idle word that men shall speak, they shall give account thereof in the day of judgment.** This is the level of idle words. The literal Greek meaning here is "nonworking."[1] These words don't do anything for you, but they don't do anything against you either.

Hebrews 12:1 tells us what to do with those kinds of words. It says, **Let us lay aside every weight, and the sin which doth so easily beset us, and let us run with patience the race that is set before us.** Now we all know what sin is. But what are the weights to which this verse is referring? They are the things that don't really hurt you, but they don't help you either. They just weigh you down and keep you from running the race of life God has called you to run. Idle words go hand in hand with those kinds of weights. Sometimes weights take the form of a hobby or recreational activity such as golf or fishing.

For me, flying airplanes was a weight at one point in my life—not that flying is a sin, because it isn't. It just occupied too much of my time and thought life. It competed with God for the priority in my heart and life. It became a weight because of the time and consideration I gave to it, and it kept me from running my spiritual race. Consequently, much of the talking I did revolved around flying. Because I was a pilot, I loved to get together with other pilots and talk about flying—airplanes, approaches, maneuvers, aerobatics and all the rest. Our conversations all centered around flying.

The more I talked about flying, the more of a weight it became to me. I was speaking idle words. They weren't bad words; they were just unproductive words. They weren't promoting the purpose of God. They weren't releasing the angelic host. They didn't hurt me, but they didn't bring the life of God to me either.

As you go through your day, you will have many opportunities to speak idle words. Whether it is some current event in the news or something else that has attracted your attention, these are occasions that inspire idle, nonworking words. And Jesus said that one day you will give an account for your words in the Day of Judgment.

This doesn't literally mean that someone is taking down every word you say and that you are going to give account for every word that didn't work to promote God's purpose in your life. No, at the judgment seat of Christ, you will give an account of the deeds done in this earthly body. And the things you do are ultimately a product of the words you speak. It is all tied together.

Out of the abundance of the heart, the mouth speaks and gives direction to our lives. (Matthew 12:34.) The Lord even says that the idle words, the nonworking words, will produce idle, nonproductive behavior. And when you stand before the judgment seat of Christ one day to receive the rewards for the things you have done on this earth, you will have to give account for all of the wasted time.

Does this mean you can never talk about your hobbies? Of course not. It is quite possible for you to talk about those things in your life that are fun and enjoyable without speaking idle words. When you are out on the golf course or the fishing stream, you can praise God for the beautiful day and the hole in one and the twelve-inch rainbow trout you caught. Then your words become something that contributes to the purpose of God.

Personally, I had to lay down my flying for a while in order to get it into the proper place in my life. I gave it up for several years. When I had grown enough in the Lord to be able to accommodate that interest without it weighing me down, God brought it back into my life.

Today it is a great blessing to me, but it doesn't occupy all of my thought life. And when I am flying, the praises of God are in my heart and on my lips. My copilot and I talk about what a blessing of God it is to be flying at 41,000 feet and to look down on the clouds or see the sun rising in the distance. We talk about how God has blessed us to be able to get from point A to point B in this manner. Our words, although relating to that particular activity, are no longer idle or nonworking words. They are words that glorify God. They lift Him up. They give Him credit. In short, they are words of life.

Don't Murmur and Complain
• • •

The fourth level of words you encounter as you descend lower on the scale from life to death can be seen in 1 Corinthians 10:10: **Neither murmur ye, as some of them also murmured, and were destroyed of the destroyer.** That verse is talking about the children of Israel who wandered and died after forty years in the wilderness. Verse 11 goes on to say: **Now all these things happened** unto them for ensamples: and they are written for our admonition, *upon whom the ends of the world are come.*

Of course, we are the ones who are living in the end time. This verse is speaking specifically to you and me! The example of the Israelites in the wilderness is given to us so we will understand the power that words have to thwart the will of God for our lives. The Israelites were the people of God, recipients of a wonderful miracle of deliverance from bondage in Egypt.

They witnessed the plagues against Egypt and, later, the destruction of the great Egyptian army. They had crossed over a large sea as though on dry ground. God supernaturally brought them manna and quail to eat. Their clothes didn't wear out. They watched as bitter water became sweet and drinkable. They saw miracle after miracle. But they never made it to the land of promise. They never made it to the land that flowed with milk and honey.

The Promised Land was God's will for them. He had heard their cries and brought them out of bondage, but they missed what God had prepared for them. Why? Because they murmured and complained continually.

There is a place God has planned for each of us, a divinely appointed destiny that flows with milk and honey. But if we make the same mistake the children of Israel made, then we, too, can die outside the promise of God, outside the will of God and outside His blessing. We can die in the wilderness and never know what it would have been like to experience the life of God on this earth.

So we need to learn from the example of the children of Israel. We need to pay attention to the instructions God gave them—instructions like the one found in Exodus 23:20,21:

> Behold, I send an Angel before thee, to keep
> thee in the way, and to bring thee into the place
> which I have prepared. Beware of him, and obey
> his voice, provoke him not; for he will not pardon
> your transgressions: for my name is in him.

Earlier in this book we discussed the role that angels play in God's plan. We saw that they are messengers of His grace and blessing and that they don't have the ability to forgive or to arbitrarily extend grace. This is what the children of Israel were being warned about in the above verse. But many didn't heed that warning. As Hebrews 3:16 says, **For some, when they had heard, did provoke.**

What did the Israelites do to provoke the angel God sent them to lead them in the way? They murmured and complained. And because of their continual murmuring and complaining, they provoked the angel of the Lord and completely missed out on the blessing God had prepared for them.

That account is in the Bible as an example to keep us from making the same mistake. It is warning us not to provoke our angels and miss out on what God has destined for us.

You will want to make sure that grumbling, complaining and murmuring aren't part of your vocabulary. Those are the words that comprise level four, and it is a bad level to be on because it opens you to death. Of course, you will still have your salvation, and heaven will still be your home. But the touch of death can seriously affect you in this natural life, and the blessings of God will forever escape you if you murmur and complain.

DANGEROUS WORDS
• • •

Finally, we come to the fifth level of words. This is the lowest level and the one that you certainly want to avoid. It is the level of words that brings death. These are the words that are totally contrary to the Word of God and the words of life. The Bible says that God and His Word are one. (John 1:1.) When you speak words contrary to the Word of God, you are speaking against God Himself.

Most people don't even have a conscious understanding of this truth. There are two kinds of angels out there that hearken to a person's words. One is the good and godly angelic host who hearkens to the voice of God's Word; the others are the fallen angels. Like the godly angels, fallen angels were created to respond to words as well. That is how they function. That is how they operate.

So the next time you speak something contrary to the Word of God, you need to think about this. Not only have you disabled your ministering angels by failing to give voice to the Word of God, but you have commissioned the angels of the realm of darkness to do the things they want to do in your life—steal, kill and destroy. (John 10:10.)

But God wants you to be protected from these things. That is why the Word says in Ephesians 4:29, **Let no corrupt communication proceed out of your mouth.** Corrupt words are those that are contrary to the Word of God. Just as you put voice to God's Word by speaking words of life, you put voice to the power of the enemy by speaking corrupt words.

Verse 31 of the same chapter reaffirms this idea when it says, **Let all bitterness, and wrath, and anger, and**

clamour, and evil speaking, be put away from you, with all malice. Evil speaking, wrath and anger, all born out of a bitter heart, work together to corrupt the purpose of God. Evil speaking keeps the ministering angels from fulfilling their assignment on your behalf. It is no coincidence that verse 27 warns us, **Neither give place to the devil,** because every time you say something counter to the Word of God, you are giving place or access to the devil and his demons in your life.

One, Two, Three, Four, Five
· · ·

Before we leave the subject of words, let's review the five levels or categories of words and how they affect the angels working on your behalf. First, put voice to the Word of God and be diligent to act on His Word in your life. This is level number one.

If you can't do that, or if you aren't strong enough yet in your faith, keep doing what the Word of God says and just don't say anything until you can put voice to His Word. Use the vocabulary of silence. This is level two.

Then beware of the idle words in your life. These are the nonworking words that won't necessarily hurt you, but they won't help you either. They are the weights that keep you from running your race. These are the nonproductive words of level three.

Then there are the level-four words. These are the words of murmuring and complaining that we speak when things aren't going our way or when we don't understand what God is doing in our lives. We need to heed the warning given to the children of Israel and not provoke our angel.

We don't want to die out in the wilderness and miss the promised blessing and purpose of God.

Finally, there is level five. These are the words that are contrary to the Word of God. When you speak these words, death has entry into your life. You immobilize your ministering angels, and you loose the angels of darkness to operate and promote evil in your life. If uncorrected, these words will drag you all the way down into spiritual death.

Remember to give proper regard to the words of your mouth. As you develop new habit patterns with regard to your speech, you will eventually speak the Word of God naturally and instinctively. Granted, it will take some practice, and you will have to catch yourself and discipline your speech for a period of time. But eventually, you will fall into a new pattern of speech that aligns the way you talk with the Word of God. You will speak words of life. You will speak forth the principles of God's Word. And as you begin to speak the blessings of the Lord and words of life, the touch of death will become less and less frequent. Most importantly, the ministry of angels on your behalf will become an active factor in your daily life.

C H A P T E R   1 1

War in the Heavenlies
•••

Now that you know why angels were created, what they do and what they respond to, I want to broaden your understanding of them even further. I want to give you a historical look at the origin of angels and the events that led to the fall of nearly a third of the hosts of heaven.

In order to do that, we first need to examine the history of the earth and creation in general. I mentioned at the beginning of this book that I would use the Bible as my primary source for study. The Bible is our only reliable resource with regard to these things because it alone establishes truth. It didn't originate in the mind of man but was divinely inspired through the mouths of hundreds of prophets and scribes over thousands of years. It is crucial that we recognize the Bible as our basic point of reference.

With that said, let's begin our discussion of creation with Genesis 1:1, **In the beginning God created the heaven and the earth.** Notice, this verse doesn't point to a definite date or a specific point in time. It references the dateless, ageless past. It just says, **In the beginning.**

I do think, however, that it is important to have a basic understanding of the time frames of creation because there are two different schools of thought regarding when the "beginning" really was. One school of thought teaches that the beginning of the earth itself coincided with the creation of Adam. Chronologically, this can be traced back 6,000 years or so. According to the "young earth" interpretation, "the beginning" refers to that point in time.

On the other hand, the scientific community through fossil records and other geological dating methods, has speculated that the universe originated somewhere in the range of fifteen billion years ago with some type of remarkable cosmic event or big bang. That, science would say, was "the beginning." According to current scientific thought, the earth as we know it was formed between four and five billion years ago. This time frame is mutually agreed upon by both secular scientists and many "old earth" creation scientists as well.

While reasonable people of faith can differ on this point, I am persuaded that the weight of biblical evidence supports the "old earth" view. Let me explain why.

First, let's take a look at Genesis 1:1. It states that in the beginning, somewhere in the dateless past, God created the heaven and the earth. What the Bible reveals here in its very first verse is the idea of universal creation. We know through physics and astrophysics how the galaxies and solar systems have been formed. God didn't just set one planet here and another planet there with nothing in between. There is a universal system that holds them all together. We can assume that the universal system came into being in Genesis 1:1.

AN ANGELIC CATASTROPHE
. . .

The Bible indicates that at the creation moment of Genesis 1:1, the angels had already been created. They were already in existence prior to the universal creation event. The book of Job bears this out when God says to Job:

> Where wast thou when I laid the foundations of the earth? declare, if thou hast understanding. Who hath laid the measures thereof, if thou knowest? or who hath stretched the line upon it? Whereupon are the foundations thereof fastened? or who laid the corner stone thereof; *When the morning stars sang together, and all the sons of God shouted for joy?*

> Job 38:4-7

The two terms *sons of God* and *morning stars* are frequently used in the Bible to refer to the angelic hosts. So we see here that the angels were present when the creation of the earth began, and they rejoiced in it!

But then something happened. Some catastrophic event must have occurred because in Genesis 1:2 we read: **And the earth was without form, and void; and darkness was on the face of the deep.** Now, the familiar phrase, **without form, and void,** is a translation of two rhyming Hebrew words—*tohu* and *bohu*. My *Hebrew-English Lexicon* defines the word *tohu* as "formlessness, confusion, unreality, emptiness, chaos or waste."[1] The word *bohu* is defined as "emptiness."[2]

Together, these two words describe a chaotic, confused mess. Interestingly, Yiddish-speaking mothers today still use the term *tohu va bohu* to describe a messy, disorganized place. Many a Jewish teenager's room has been declared *tohu va bohu* by an irate mom.

Genesis isn't the only place in the Old Testament in which this phrase is used. In the fourth chapter of Jeremiah, we find the prophet seemingly looking back to the very time described in Genesis 1:2 when he says,

> I beheld the earth, and, lo, it was without form, and void [*tohu va bohu*]; and the heavens, and they had no light. I beheld the mountains, and, lo, they trembled, and all the hills moved lightly. I beheld, and, lo, there was no man, and all the birds of the heavens were fled. I beheld, and, lo, the fruitful place was a wilderness, and all the cities thereof were broken down at the presence of the Lord, and by his fierce anger. For thus hath the Lord said, The whole land shall be desolate; yet will I not make a full end.
>
> Jeremiah 4:23-27

Did the first verse in the passage sound familiar? Just as in Genesis 1:2, we see the earth **without form, and void,** and we see darkness covering it. This passage indicates that the cause of this darkness and chaos was a great judgment of some sort. A little further along we will see what that judgment might have been, but for now, let's look back at Genesis 1:1,2.

In verse 1, we see the earth created. In verse 2, we discover that it is a chaotic, confused mess. The question arises: Is that the way God created the earth? We find a clear, unequivocal answer to that question in Isaiah 45:18: **For thus saith the Lord that created the heavens; God himself that formed the earth and made it; he hath established it, he *created it not in vain* [*tohu*], he formed it to be inhabited.**

It's no accident that the Word of God uses the same word *tohu* in this verse as it used in Genesis 1:2. This verse clearly states that God didn't create the earth *tohu*. He created it perfect and inhabitable. That means that something happened between verse 1 and verse 2, something that distorted the surface of the earth and rendered it chaotic and confused.

The earth *became* uninhabitable and dark. In fact, the original Hebrew syntax actually supports the use of the word *became* in this context rather than *was*.[3] With this knowledge, we can safely translate the first two verses of Genesis this way:

1   **In the beginning, God created the heaven and the earth.**

2   **And the earth *became* chaotic and confused, and darkness was on the face of the deep.**

In actuality, millions or even billions of years could lie between these two verses. What kind of cataclysmic event could have wreaked such havoc? The answer to that question lies with one of the three chief angels, an angel by the name of Lucifer.

LUCIFER'S FALL
• • •

As I've pointed out previously, God created the angels for the purpose of managing and administering His affairs in the universal creation. He established them in different ranks and orders and assigned to them various areas of responsibility with differing levels of authority and power.

The cherubim, for example, were designated as the ruling authority over certain physical areas of the universe. Placed over them in authority were the three archangels: Gabriel, Michael and Lucifer. Gabriel was designated as the messenger of God or the angel of the Lord. He appears in the Bible several times, most notably when he visited Zacharias in Luke 1:11-20 and announced the birth of John the Baptist and later when he visited Mary with the news of Jesus' birth in Luke 1:26-38.

On the other hand, Michael was assigned to battle. He is the warring angel. Remember the angel who appeared to Daniel after being delayed three weeks because of a battle in the spirit realm? (Daniel 10:13.) Michael was the angel who was dispatched to help this particular angel in the battle with the prince of Persia.

Then we have Lucifer. I want to spend some time discussing him because he is the one responsible for the catastrophic event that left the earth **without form, and void.**

A Long Way To Fall
...

To effectively discuss Lucifer, I must introduce a principle of biblical interpretation called "the law of double reference." Throughout Scripture, usually in the context of a prophetic utterance, the Spirit of God will address an individual when in reality He is speaking to the spirit that is prompting the individual's actions and behavior.

A good example of this is found in Matthew 16:21-23. There, Jesus had just described what He must suffer when Peter pulled Him aside and argued, **Be it far from thee, Lord: this shall not be unto thee** (v. 22). Do you remember Jesus' response? He turned to Peter and said, **Get thee behind me, Satan: thou art an offense unto me!** (v. 23). Was Jesus speaking to Peter? Yes, but in reality, He was dealing with Satan. This is the law of double reference in action.

Keeping that in mind, look at Ezekiel 28:11-15. The law of double reference can also be applied here because, even though the passage is addressed to the king of Tyrus, God is most certainly speaking about Lucifer or Satan:

> Moreover the word of the Lord came unto me, saying, Son of man, take up a lamentation upon the king of Tyrus, and say unto him, Thus saith the Lord God; Thou sealest up the sum, full of wisdom, and perfect in beauty. Thou hast been in Eden the garden of God; every precious stone was thy covering, the sardius, topaz, and the diamond, the beryl, the onyx, and the jasper, the sapphire, the emerald, and the carbuncle, and gold: the workmanship of thy tabrets and of thy pipes was prepared in thee in the day that thou wast created.
>
> Thou art the anointed cherub that covereth; and I have set thee so: thou wast upon the holy mountain of God; thou hast walked up and down in the midst of the stones of fire. Thou wast perfect in thy ways from the day that thou wast created, till iniquity was found in thee.

Obviously, this doesn't strictly apply to the historical king of Tyrus. Although he was, in fact, an evil king, in this passage God is addressing the spirit behind the king of Tyrus—the archangel called Lucifer. Here are a few of the things we learn about Lucifer from this passage.

He was **the anointed cherub that covereth.** This means he had been anointed to rule. Apparently, Lucifer was second only to God in his authority, a position not given to any other angel in Scripture. He was perfect in beauty and full of wisdom. He had special physical features which produced the sound of tabrets and pipes. We have reason to believe that because of these, he was responsible for praise and worship and the music in heaven.

Lucifer was a marvelous creature. He was the apex of God's creation to that point. He was covered with every beautiful, glimmering stone and with gold as though they were a garment. He was perfect in all his ways from the day he was created until the day iniquity was found in him.

But I want you to see something else that is said about Lucifer. Verse 13 says, **Thou hast been in Eden the garden of God.** The Bible says he walked in the Garden of Eden as a beautiful and majestic creature, yet we see him in Genesis 3:1 in the Garden of Eden as a serpent, more subtle than any creature God had made. How do we reconcile these two dramatically different views of him?

One way is to consider that they refer to Satan as he was in two different time frames! The account in Ezekiel may very well describe him as he was in the dateless past when he was perfect in all his ways and when he led the worship and praise that filled the heavens. God had appointed him to rule the universal creation as second in command. And at that point, it seems that Lucifer made the planet earth his headquarters and operated out of the Garden of Eden. This would have been millions of years before he met Adam as a serpent in the Genesis account.

Lucifer's glory days took place long before the earth became without form and void. At that time, earth was an inhabited place, and Lucifer was the ultimate authority there. He was second in command only to God and even now is still referred to as the god of this world. (1 Corinthians 4:4.) He was a brilliant and beautiful creature who could transform himself into an angel of light. (2 Corinthians 11:14.) In Isaiah 14:12, he is referred to as the *son of the morning*. Even his name, *Lucifer*, means "morning star."[4]

92

That is why, when we encounter evil, it isn't likely to come in the form of a ghost or goblin. As a matter of fact, we need to get rid of the traditional view of Satan as some grotesque, horrible being with horns who is clothed in a bright red jumpsuit and holding a pitchfork!

Unfortunately, however, this marvelous creature determined to exalt himself above God. Isaiah 14:13,14 reveals the intent of his heart when it tells us,

> For thou hast said in thine heart, I will ascend into heaven, I will exalt my throne above the stars of God: I will sit also upon the mount of the congregation, in the sides of the north: I will ascend above the heights of the clouds; I will be like the most High.

As a result, God says in Ezekiel 28:17 that He will cast him to the ground:

> Thine heart was lifted up because of thy beauty, thou hast corrupted thy wisdom by reason of thy brightness: I will cast thee to the ground, I will lay thee before kings, that they may behold thee.

Then in Isaiah 14:12, God says that as a result of Lucifer's fall the nations would be weakened.

> How art thou fallen from heaven, O Lucifer, son of the morning! how art thou cut down to the ground, which didst weaken the nations!

He also says that the world would be made a wilderness, and the cities would be destroyed. (Isaiah 14:17.)

ARCHAEOLOGY DOESN'T CONTRADICT SCRIPTURE
· · ·

Now, you may be thinking to yourself, *If this is all happening in the dateless past, sometime before the creation of Adam, then why do these scripture references mention kings, cities and nations? Wouldn't that imply that there were people on the earth at that time?*

As a matter of fact, it would! Although one doesn't want to get dogmatic on this point, many Bible texts do support the existence of a pre-Adamic civilization. This, of course, would go a long way toward explaining numerous archeological discoveries of different life forms and evidence that a fruitful civilized world existed tens of thousands of years ago.

For example, consider the issue of dinosaurs and the bones of other kinds of strange creatures that archeologists have unearthed. There is room for all of that in the Bible. But beyond that, there may have been intelligent life in this distant era before Genesis 1:2—life that was organized into communities, cities and even nations.

Adam was the first of a new kind of creation. Adam was different because he was created in the image and likeness of God. (Genesis 1:26.) Nothing had ever been created with that distinction before.

It is important to realize that this Godlikeness goes beyond our physical appearance because even angels and other beings can take on the appearance of man. It isn't just because of the way we look; it is our spiritual nature and capacity that makes us unique in all of creation.

We are the first and only species created that can actually be joined with the Spirit of God. We can be one with God, and God can indwell us. We can draw upon the very power and anointing of God that raised Jesus from the dead and created this universe. That is what makes us in the image and likeness of God. So when Adam was created six thousand years ago, that is what came into being—a new, Godlike creature that never existed before.

Personally, I agree with those who believe that, prior to Adam's creation, there was a race of manlike creatures on the earth who were capable of developing communities and cities. These manlike creatures most probably made up the nations referred to in Isaiah 14:12.

What happened to this pre-Adamic civilization and its inhabitants? I'm convinced they were all destroyed in the rebellion and fall of Lucifer. Revelation 12:7 speaks of that destruction when it says,

> **And there was war in heaven: Michael and his angels fought against the dragon; and the dragon fought and his angels.**

Based on Revelation 12:4, it seems that Lucifer was able to gather a third of the angelic host to assist him in his rebellion. But verses 8 and 9 say:

> [They] **prevailed not; neither was their place found any more in heaven. And the great dragon was cast out, that old serpent, called the Devil, and Satan, which deceiveth the whole world: he was cast out into the earth, and his angels were cast out with him.**

This cosmic conflict took place long before Adam came on the scene. Obviously, whatever civilization existed on the earth at that time was deceived and became part of the rebellion. As a result, Satan and his angels were cast down onto the earth. That is why verse 12 says,

> **Therefore rejoice, ye heavens, and ye that dwell in them. Woe to the inhabiters of the earth and of the sea! for the devil is come down unto you, having great wrath, because he knoweth that he hath but a short time.**

This is the great catastrophic event that destroyed the earth and left it *tohu va bohu*—without form and void.

Remember Jeremiah's vision of this judgment event from Jeremiah 4:23-26? The prophet described how the earth was without form and void and how the mountains trembled. He recounts that there was no man and that the birds had all fled. Then he says in verse 26,

I beheld, and, lo, the fruitful place was a wilderness, and all the cities thereof were broken down at the presence of the Lord, and by his fierce anger.

He was looking at the earth as we might see it in Genesis 1:2. It was a messed-up place. The cities were all destroyed. Why? Because Satan had lost the battle waged in the heavens and was cast back onto the earth.

THE ANGELS WHO KEPT NOT THEIR FIRST ESTATE
• • •

In addition to providing us with insight into the history of Lucifer and the fallen angels, the Bible also sheds light on their destiny. For instance, 2 Peter 2:4 says, **God spared not the angels that sinned, but cast them down to hell, and delivered them into chains of darkness, to be reserved unto judgment.**

This verse makes it seem as if all the angels of the rebellion are chained down in hell and in darkness waiting for the final judgment. But they can't all be down there because, if that were the case, Satan would have to be there too. And we know he isn't because the Bible says he moves about as a roaring lion throughout the whole earth, seeking whom he may devour. (1 Peter 5:8.) He couldn't be doing that if he was chained in hell. So we must conclude that only some of the angels who rebelled have been chained in darkness. But which ones are they?

Jude 1:6 seems to shed some light on this question when it says, **And the angels** *which kept not their first estate,* **but left their own habitation, he hath reserved in everlasting chains under darkness unto the judgment of the great day.** Although all of the fallen angels rebelled, Peter says that some of them did something worse—they **kept not their first estate.**

Genesis 6:1,2 indicates what that may mean. At the time, approximately 1,400 years had already passed since Adam had been created and had begun to multiply on the earth. The effects of sin were beginning to be felt, and verse 2 says, **The sons of God saw the daughters of men that they were fair; and they took them wives of all which they chose.**

As I said before, **sons of God** is a phrase used to describe angels. We see here that some of the fallen angels were beginning to take human women as wives. As a result, Genesis 6:4 tells us:

> **There were giants in the earth in those days; and also after that, when the sons of God came in unto the daughters of men, and they bare children to them, the same became mighty men which were of old, men of renown.**

This may have happened because, after man's fall in the Garden of Eden, God had declared that the seed of man would crush the head of the serpent. (Genesis 3:15.) Of course, Satan tried to stop that from happening by trying to genetically alter man's offspring through cohabitation with human women. It seems that Satan's goal was to make man even more genetically predisposed to choose evil.[5]

So after the fallen angels cohabited with human women, they produced physically abnormal offspring described as giants. That in itself was bad enough. But in the eyes of God, something even worse had happened. Satan had tampered with the right of man to choose good and evil, and that is where God drew the line. He condemned those angels who had **kept not their first estate** and moved into the area of procreation, which was reserved for the human species.[6]

Again, this is just one opinion on the subject. Even though one can't be extremely dogmatic on the matter, it does seem to answer quite a few questions, especially those pertaining to the Flood. Most probably Noah and his family were the only ones who hadn't been affected by Satan's scheme. The Flood, then, was God's way of stopping Satan's effort to poison the seed of man.[7]

MAN, A FREE MORAL AGENT
• • •

We have taken a closer look at some doctrines that aren't essential to your eternal salvation in an attempt to explain a few things with regard to the fall of Lucifer and its effect on mankind. What this perspective says to me more than anything else is that God won't allow the satanic host to override our free moral agency. God has created us in His image and given us the choice of life or death, blessing or cursing. Even Lucifer had that choice. But pride confused his wisdom, and he was deceived in his own heart.

When Satan tried to override our free will in order to force us to do evil, he was held in check by the Most High God. It is good to know that even Satan is forced to respect our moral freedom. And it is even better to know that God is always and forever protecting us!

Satan's Subtle Second Word

• • •

As we have seen, there had been a lot of action in the spirit realm before Adam was ever created. Lucifer had gotten too big for his britches. He had rebelled against God and taken a third of the angels with him in that rebellion. These became the angels of darkness—the fallen angels. Their sole purpose now was to prevent the blessing of God from flowing to mankind because it was the only way they could possibly forestall their own dark, eternal destiny.

These fallen angels know the Word. They know the prophecies that have been spoken against them. They know that the lake of fire is their ultimate destination. (Revelation 20:14,15.) So they try to postpone that day by keeping the will of God from happening in your life and mine; their goal is to keep us from experiencing God's promised blessings.

Now my point is this: Just as surely as God's angels are commissioned to minister His blessings to you, the fallen angels work with all diligence to hinder those blessings. And if you are going to assist God's angels and frustrate the devil's crew, you will have to be able to distinguish between them.

At times that can be more difficult than you may think because Satan aspires to be like God. He tries to emulate or counterfeit Him, even today. According to 2 Corinthians 11:14, he can be transformed into an angel of light. Therefore, sometimes the difference between the two kinds of angelic hosts are very subtle. [If we are going to success-fully identify these differences between God's angels and fallen angels, we must understand something about the strategies and tactics Satan and the fallen angels use to work against us.]

UNDERSTANDING SATAN'S STRATEGIES
• • •

One of the first things we need to know is that Lucifer and his fallen angels are neither omnipresent (all-present), omnipotent (all-powerful) or omniscient (all-knowing). This is an important point to understand because many believers seem to unconsciously ascribe these traits to them. But the truth is, fallen angels are none of these things.

Lucifer is an angelic being and can't be in more than one place at one time. He can't be harassing you and, at the same time, be harassing some unfortunate man over in China. The devil doesn't have that ability. Rather, he has to rely upon delegated authority. His angels have levels of rank and file just as the angels of God do. There are different orders of authority and assignments of responsibility in the kingdom of darkness. We see an overview of this hierarchy in Ephesians 6:12:

> **For we wrestle not against flesh and blood, but against principalities, against powers, against the rulers of the darkness of this world, against spiritual wickedness in high places.**

Satan has to rely upon the input he gets from his proxies because he can't be everywhere at once.

We have seen in the Word that God assigns angels to you to keep you in your way and to take charge over you. (Psalm 91:11.) But be aware that there are also demonic angels on assignment *against* you. As your visibility in the kingdom of God increases—as the anointing on your life and your knowledge of the Word grows—you become a greater threat to the kingdom of darkness. As a result, the devil assigns more resources against you.

Although Lucifer and his wicked host aren't all-powerful, they *are* supernatural and have supernatural strength. Don't underestimate their abilities because, in their realm, they are powerful creatures. You are no match for them unless, of course, you are in Christ.

The Bible says, **Greater is he that is in you, than he that is in the world** (1 John 4:4). That is part of the good news of the Gospel. But without the Lord, without the power of God, you wouldn't have a chance against the demonic host.

Another fact you need to know is that Lucifer isn't omniscient. He doesn't know what you are thinking. That is why the demons assigned against you are so interested in hearing what you say and seeing what you do. The devil has no idea what goes on inside your head. He has to wait until you tell him or show him. Once you do that, he shapes his strategy against you accordingly.

Let's say that you are afraid of flying, for instance. A demonic spirit doesn't know that until you verbally say so. Once he is aware of it, however, he can begin magnifying that fear. He might send various people to you who want to talk about the dangers of flying or about news of some recent plane crash. He will use those people to feed the fear in you so it will grow.

Fear and faith operate on the same principles. Just as faith is believing in God's ability to bless you, fear is believing in the enemy's ability to do you harm. And just as faith draws good things to you, fear will cause the very things you fear to come upon you.

Satan will also watch for negative patterns in your behavior. When he sees one, he will make sure you get additional opportunities to pursue that negative behavior. For instance, if he sees that you always lose your temper in a certain situation, he will bring that situation back time and again in hopes that your anger will flare.

I used to wonder why, with all of the illegal drugs that are being peddled in our culture, nobody ever tried to sell me any of the stuff. Then I realized that drug use isn't a demonstrated weakness for me. It never has been. The devil knows I wouldn't be tempted to buy it, so he doesn't bother to send it my way. On the other hand, a former drug addict will have somebody trying to sell him drugs every time he turns around. Is that a coincidence? No! It is the demonic host at work in the unseen realm.

Of course, as I pointed out in the last chapter, God won't allow that evil host to impose their will upon a person because man was created as a free moral agent. God has already locked up the angels who tried to tamper with man's free will. Satan knows that if he wants to remain loose on this earth, he can't force evil on anybody. His only tool is deception. It is the only thing he can legally use.

Of course, no one deliberately chooses death. A person must be deceived first. Therefore, Satan's only viable strategy is to trick that person into making a wrong choice.

When it comes to deceiving unbelievers, his approach is very simple: keep them out of church and keep them away from Christians. Period. That is all that is necessary to keep them moving down the path to destruction.

That is why the devil spends relatively little time on unbelievers. They are, by default, subject to the curse that is in this earth. That curse entered through Adam when he sinned and has been working here ever since. Just look at the world around you, and you can see that for yourself! It is filled with infirmity, famine, heartache, pain—and, most of all, death. Satan doesn't need to spend that much time beating up a nonbeliever because the curse in the earth is already doing that. Therefore, he just does what is necessary to make sure they keep on being unbelievers.

In Hosea 4:6, God says, **My people are destroyed for lack of knowledge.** If Satan can keep unbelievers from knowing the truth found in the Word, then the truth can't set them free. (John 8:32.) He has them right where he wants them—outside the church!

The Second Word in the Garden
• • •

When it comes to the believer, the one whose life is hid in Christ, the enemy has an entirely different plan of attack. Believers have heard the Word of God. They have access to the truth through the Bible, the indwelling Holy Spirit and anointed preaching and teaching. So the enemy must work much harder to promote deception in their lives.

Very simply, if you are a believer, Satan's strategy is to bring you a second word or second opinion, so to speak, that differs from what the first word, the Word of God, says on a given subject. Let me illustrate what I mean. Look at Genesis 3:1-6,

> Now the serpent was more subtil than any beast of the field which the Lord God had made. And he said unto the woman, Yea, hath God said, Ye shall not eat of every tree of the garden? And the woman said unto the serpent, We may eat of the fruit of the trees of the garden: But of the fruit of the tree which is in the midst of the garden, God hath said, Ye shall not eat of it, neither shall ye touch it, lest ye die. And the serpent said unto the woman, Ye shall not surely die: For God doth know that in the day ye eat thereof, then your eyes shall be opened, and ye shall be as gods, knowing good and evil.
>
> And when the woman saw that the tree was good for food, and that it was pleasant to the eyes, and a tree to be desired to make one wise, she took of the fruit thereof, and did eat, and gave also unto her husband with her; and he did eat.

God's first word on the subject had been delivered in the previous chapter when He said, **But of the tree of the knowledge of good and evil, thou shalt not eat of it: for in the day that thou eatest thereof thou shalt surely die** (Genesis 2:17). The Word of the Lord on this subject was clear. But Satan, who was more subtle than any other creature in creation, managed to bring a second word and tricked Adam and Eve into heeding it. They were deceived, plain and simple.

GOD'S WORD IS QUESTIONED
• • •

It is important to examine the above passage of Scripture carefully because there are four red flags in it that will help you learn to identify the deception of the second word before you fall for it. Any deception the enemy tries to perpetrate in your life will probably carry one or more of these red-flag characteristics.

The first red flag we invariably see when a second word comes is that it begins with a question. In the above example that question was, **Hath God said, Ye shall not eat of every tree of the garden?** (Genesis 3:1). As is usually the case, the enemy's question challenges the authority of what God said. If you aren't firm and clear about what God's Word says, you are vulnerable to being led down this progressive path to deception.

Eve didn't have God's words of instruction clearly imbedded in her heart. She made this clear in her response to the serpent. She said, **We may eat of the fruit of the trees of the garden: But of the fruit of the tree which is** *in the midst of the garden,* **God hath said, Ye shall not eat of it,** *neither shall ye touch it,* **lest ye die.**

God didn't say that. The tree **in the midst of the garden,** as described in Genesis 2:9, was the tree of life. It stood alongside the tree of the knowledge of good and evil. But God didn't say, "Don't eat of the tree in the midst of the garden." In fact, He commanded them that they *should* eat of the tree of life. Neither had God said anything about not *touching* the tree.

The fact that Eve didn't know exactly what God had said is significant. It is a red flag on the road to deception.

Don't be too hard on Eve, though. God had instructed Adam about these things and apparently he hadn't done a very good job of passing those instructions on to his newly-formed bride. The fact that God's first word was fuzzy in Eve's mind enabled the deception of the second word to continue.

GOD'S WORD IS CONTRADICTED
AND HIS CHARACTER MALIGNED
...

The next two red flags on the path towards deception begin with an innocent question and turn into an outright contradiction of God's Word that involves the questioning of God's character. The questioning comes from the devil, who takes a shot at God by saying: **Ye shall not surely die: For God doth know that in the day ye eat thereof, then your eyes shall be opened, and ye shall be as gods, knowing good and evil** (Genesis 3:4,5). The devil implied that God was withholding something really good from them. This is another warning flag in the process of deception.

To avoid the devil's trap, you must know that the Word says God is good and has your best interest at heart. This is imperative. If you don't study the Word and let it get down deep into your spirit, then you run the risk of having it twisted into a contradiction. You also open yourself to doubts about the character of God.

AN APPEAL TO THE FLESH
...

The last red flag in the process of deception was an appeal to the flesh. Genesis 3:6 says, **And when the woman**

saw that the tree was good for food, and that it was pleasant to the eyes, and a tree to be desired to make one wise, she took of the fruit thereof, and did eat. This last step in Satan's plan was directed toward a fleshly desire. He offered Adam and Eve something that would appease the flesh, something their carnal nature desired. That carnal nature is a part of us that we all have to deal with on a regular, daily basis. And it is a major factor in any deception that occurs.

THE SECOND WORD OF A PROPHET
• • •

Now that we have laid the foundation, I want to show you another example of the second word. This example is taken from a story found in First Kings 13:1-7. The story begins with a young prophet, a man of God, who had come out of Judah at the prompting of the Lord to go to the town of Bethel.

He had been sent to Bethel to prophesy against an evil king named Jeroboam. King Jeroboam had torn down the temples and the places where God was worshipped, and in their place the king had erected his own altars to golden images and false gods. As the young prophet cried out against the altars, he declared a sign would be given to verify that his words were from God. The sign was that the altars would be split into two and the ashes upon them would be poured out.

King Jeroboam happened to be near one of these altars as the prophet cried out. When he heard what the prophet said, King Jeroboam reached out with his hand to grab the young prophet and stop him. But as he did, his hand withered instantly, and he was unable to use it. At the same time, the altars were split in two, and their ashes were poured out on the ground just as the prophet had said.

Jeroboam then begged for the prophet to pray to God for his hand to be restored. The young prophet agreed, and after he prayed, the king's hand was healed. Then Jeroboam invited the young prophet to his house that he might be rewarded and refreshed with food and drink.

All this is recorded as a wonderful demonstration of what happens when a person obeys the Word of the Lord—the first word. When we respond to the Word of God, when we put voice to His Word, the kingdom of God gains greater visibility, the high places of the enemy are torn down and we enjoy supernatural safety in dangerous situations. Notice that when the king stretched forth his hand to bring harm to the young prophet, God supernaturally intervened. Divine protection goes with us as we obey the first word of the Lord.

Let's pick up the story again in verse 7, where the king invited the young prophet to come home with him for refreshment:

> And the king said unto the man of God, Come home with me, and refresh thyself, and I will give thee a reward. And the man of God said unto the king, If thou wilt give me half thine house, I will not go in with thee, neither will I eat bread nor drink water in this place: For so was it charged me by the word of the Lord, saying, Eat no bread, nor drink water, nor turn again by the same way that thou camest. So he went another way, and returned not by the way that he came to Bethel.
>
> 1 Kings 13:7-10

We see here that the young prophet had received a word from the Lord. He had been told not to eat or drink there, and he obeyed that word. But in the next few verses, something unexpected happens. It is here we see the deceptive nature of the second word as an old, fellow prophet from that area follows the young prophet and makes him another offer:

> Come home with me, and eat bread. And he [the young prophet] said, I may not return with thee, nor go in with thee: neither will I eat bread nor drink water with thee in this place: For it was said to me by the word of the Lord, Thou shalt eat no bread nor drink water there, nor turn again to go by the way that thou camest.
>
> He said unto him, I am a prophet also as thou art; and an angel spake unto me by the word of the Lord, saying, Bring him back with thee into thine house, that he may eat bread and drink water. But he lied unto him.
>
> So he went back with him, and did eat bread in his house, and drank water. And it came to pass, after he had eaten bread, and after he had drunk, that he saddled for him the ass, to wit, for the prophet whom he had brought back. And when he was gone, a lion met him by the way, and slew him.
>
> 1 Kings 13:15-19,23,24

There is a lot we can learn from this account, because it demonstrates the subtlety of the second word. After the word of the Lord was given to the young prophet, it was questioned twice—once by Jeroboam when he told the young prophet to come to his house and eat, and again by the old prophet who said the same thing. And to his credit, the young prophet declined firmly in both instances.

109

But then what happened? Just as in the Garden with Eve, the first word was contradicted. The old prophet told him that God had changed His mind. The angel of the Lord had instructed him not to go to the old prophet's house. No doubt, the new instructions were appealing. After all, the young prophet was hot and tired. He had come a long way and had a long way to go. He hadn't eaten. He hadn't had anything to drink. Just as in the Garden, this second word contained a powerful appeal to his flesh. He needed rest and refreshment. He yielded, and it cost him his life.

It makes you wonder what kind of angel it was that came to the old prophet, doesn't it? And what about that lion? First Peter 5:8 says, **Be sober, be vigilant; because your adversary the devil, as a roaring lion, walketh about, seeking whom he may devour.** Satan is out there walking about, seeking those whom he *may* devour. He can't devour any believer he pleases.

You have to give the devil permission before he can destroy you. You have to be deceived into walking out from under God's protective umbrella through disobedience to His Word.

But this is the process that leads to deception and, ultimately, to being devoured by the enemy. He invariably will bring a subtle second word. It is the only thing he can use to promote his evil agenda on the earth. That is why we are told to be sober and vigilant.

YOUR FIRST LINE OF DEFENSE
...

Your first line of defense against the deceptive tactics of fallen angels is to know the Word. Study it and meditate on it. Read it continuously, and let it get down deep in you. Then, be aware of the four red flags that indicate a possible second-word attack. Whether through a friend, relative, newscaster or stranger, be on the alert when the Word is questioned, when it is contradicted, when God's character is maligned or when an appeal is made to your flesh. If you do, then you will be able to distinguish between the angel of the Lord and the angel of the enemy every time.

Promise of Protection
•••

More than any other single chapter of the Bible, Psalm 91 reveals what the heavenly hosts can do in your life. It is a wonderful, scriptural picture of God's care, love and provision for your every need. Furthermore, it is a beautiful promise of His protection that reveals how He has ordained the ministry of angels to bring His blessings into your life.

FELLOWSHIP IS THE KEY
•••

First of all, this psalm does a masterful job of putting the ministry of angels into proper perspective. It reveals not only how angels serve us but also what we must do to appropriate that service. It begins with the assertion that *fellowship* is the basis for every good thing listed in the psalm: **He that dwelleth in the secret place of the most High shall abide under the shadow of the Almighty.**

Fellowship with God is the most fundamental prerequisite for angelic ministry in your life. It is the key that opens the door to God's blessings and the angels who bring those blessings. *Dwelleth* means "to dwell, sit, abide, inhabit, remain."[1] It doesn't mean "occasionally visits." To dwell in the secret place of the Most High doesn't mean spending fifteen or twenty minutes with God every now and then. It means you fellowship with Him deeply and intimately every day.

There is a difference between *relationship* with God and *fellowship* with Him. Many Christians assume that because they have a relationship with God, they are automatically in fellowship with Him. But that isn't necessarily true.

I have three children, two boys and a girl. I am their father, and they are my children. Nothing will ever change that relationship. Even if I didn't see them for twenty years, didn't talk with them, didn't even write them a letter, I would still be their father, and they would still be my children. It doesn't matter if they are good children or bad, our relationship is still father and sons and father and daughter. That won't ever change.

If, however, I don't see my children or hear from them for twenty years, I'm obviously not in fellowship with them. I don't know them, and they don't know me. Even though the relationship is intact, the fellowship isn't.

The same thing applies to our relationship and fellowship with the Father God. When we are born again, we are adopted into the family of God through the blood of His Son Jesus Christ. (Romans 8:15-17.) We become the children of God, and He becomes our Father. That is relationship. Nothing can change that. On the other hand, our fellowship with God is something different.

When you are in fellowship with somebody, you know their heart and mind. You communicate with them. There is interchange and dialogue, a sharing of heart. That is the essence of fellowship. When you are in fellowship with somebody, you know what they are thinking. You know who they are and where they stand. You know what they believe.

The same thing is true when you are in fellowship with God the Father. You know what He thinks about your life. You know His heart and His mind. You have talked to Him, and He has talked with you. You have been with Him in the secret place. That secret place is a place with God that nobody knows about but you. You are the only one that knows you have been there—except, of course, the Lord. This is where you and the Father commune with one another. And there is no mistake about it. When you are there, you know it.

We all get to that place in different ways because we are all unique individuals. But when you are in the presence of the Lord in your secret place, there is no mistaking it. And when you continue in that place, this verse says you will abide under the shadow of the Almighty.

As I've read the Bible, I've discovered that the word *shadow* is frequently used in reference to the anointing or power of God.[2] For instance, in Luke 1:26-35, the angel Gabriel went to Mary and told her she would bear a son. When Mary expressed confusion about how that could happen, Gabriel said to her: **The Holy Ghost shall come upon thee, and the power of the Highest shall overshadow thee** (Luke 1:35).

The term *shadow* is even used as a reference point for the anointing that flows through human vessels.[3] In Acts 5:15, we are told that the passing of Peter's shadow healed the sick. Again, this is referring to the anointing and power of God. When we dwell in the secret place of the Most High, that place of fellowship, we abide or remain in the shadow of the anointing and power of the Lord.

MAKE HIM YOUR REFUGE AND FORTRESS
...

Psalm 91:2 goes on to say, **I will say of the Lord, He is my refuge and my fortress: my God; in him will I trust.** Not everyone can honestly say those things about God. Only the ones who are in continual fellowship with the Lord can say those things. If a person doesn't abide in the secret place with Him, he isn't going to be heard frequently declaring, "The Lord is my refuge, in Him will I trust!"

The Hebrew word translated *refuge* here is defined simply as "a place of refuge, shelter, trust."[4] If you want to know where you are in the Lord, you can find out by getting honest with yourself and identifying your normal place of refuge. When things get tough in your life, when the pressure is great, where do you hide?

A lot of people use liquor as their hiding place. Alcohol is their refuge when their world gets rough. Others may turn on the television and vegetate for three or four hours. That becomes their escape from the difficulties of life. Others instantly run to friends or family.

What is your refuge? If you are in close fellowship with the Lord, you will say, **He is my refuge and my fortress: my God; in Him will I trust!**

But He won't only be your *refuge;* He will be your *fortress* too. When placed together in a pair, these two words essentially represent God's answer to both the small and large challenges in your life. A refuge is a secure place, a little hiding place. A fortress, on the other hand, is a large place like a castle or a stronghold. By using these two terms, the psalmist is telling you that whether you need just a little or a lot of help, God is there for you.

HE WILL DELIVER YOU

· · ·

And when God is your fortress, verse 3 becomes true for you: **Surely he shall deliver thee from the snare of the fowler, and from the noisome pestilence.** Deliverance will be a fact in your life. He will deliver you from **the snare of the fowler** and **the noisome pestilence.**

The *fowler* in Old Testament times was "one who took birds by means of nets, snares, decoys, etc." Amateur fowlers would pursue their game in the thickets and fell them with a throw-stick made of heavy wood. Often they would also take with them a decoy bird. In order to keep the decoy near its post, they usually chose a female bird and kept her nest with its eggs in the boat.[5] This is analogous to Satan. He is the spiritual fowler who uses any means he can to trip you up in your walk with God. He may even try to tether you to him by stealing your young.

The *noisome pestilence* is an odd-sounding phrase that means a "rushing, calamitous plague."[6] What does the pairing of these two terms, *fowler* and *noisome pestilence,* tell us? That whether it is a subtle trap set to snare you unaware or the enemy coming in like a flood, you can depend on God to deliver you.

HE WILL PROTECT YOU
. . .

The first part of verse 4 brings us another promise, **He shall cover thee with his feathers, and under his wings shalt thou trust.** This verse is referring to the eagle. This isn't unusual, since the Bible frequently uses the eagle as a metaphor depicting the traits and character of God. When you do a little research into the ways of eagles, you discover how appropriate this is.

For example, we know that when a storm comes, adult eagles don't flee from the storm. They don't take shelter. Instead, they face the storm and let the updrafts that come before it lift them above the storm. If they have baby eaglets in the nest, however, they remain in the nest and cover their young with the feathers of their wings.[7]

Likewise, when the storms of life come, our Father God, like the eagle, will cover you with His feathers. He will protect you under His wings. This is precisely what the first half of verse 4 tells us. But true to the pattern, the metaphor of the eagle is paired with a second image in the second half of verse 4: **His truth shall be thy shield and buckler.**

What is **his truth?** His truth is His Word. God and His Word are one. According to this verse, when your life is based on the truth of God's Word, that Word will become like a shield and buckler for you.

The shield and the buckler were two pieces of protective equipment used by the soldiers. The buckler, although used here in a figurative sense, was smaller than the shield and used in hand to hand fighting for protection.[8] The shield was also used for protection, but it was much bigger than the buckler. The shield referenced here was large enough to cover the whole body of the soldier it protected. When an attack came, the enemy would shoot waves of arrows into the sky, and the soldier would crouch down behind his shield to keep himself from harm.[9] As before, this verse is depicting two levels of protection—one for small, concentrated attacks and one for massive onslaughts when the enemy comes in overwhelming strength.

What is the result of enjoying such multilevel protection? Verses 5 and 6 tell us:

> **Thou shalt not be afraid for the terror by night; nor for the arrow that flieth by day; nor for the pestilence that walketh in darkness; nor for the destruction that wasteth at noonday.**

It doesn't matter if you are facing a frontal assault in broad daylight or if the enemy is doing something behind your back of which you are totally unaware—either way, you are protected. This is what is implied by the terms **the arrow that flieth by day** and **the terror by night.** And make no mistake about it, very often the enemy comes at you with both!

You can be focused on some obvious crisis, and along comes a relatively small problem that catches you off guard. That is how the devil works. Yet, if you are dwelling in the secret place, it doesn't matter. God will deliver you when you are in fellowship with Him.

TRUST IN HIM
• • •

The next portion of Scripture, verse 7, is very interesting. I believe many people misinterpret the symbolism of it. It says: **A thousand shall fall at thy side, and ten thousand at thy right hand; but it shall not come nigh**

thee. Many commentaries on this verse suggest that it describes enemy attackers falling by the thousands all around you while you remain unscathed. But I don't believe that is what this verse is saying because when you are in battle, those who are at your right and left sides aren't the enemy; they are your own comrades!

Therefore, I tend to agree with those who believe this verse is describing other believers who, in the fight of faith called life, are at your side and at your right hand. The sad reality is that many of them will fall. But you can't let that stop you from trusting in God's protection. It doesn't matter how many people you know who prayed to be healed but died of cancer anyway. It doesn't matter how many good Christians you know who went bankrupt. Those things won't come nigh you if you are in fellowship with God. A thousand other believers may fall, but, as a dweller in the secret place, you will remain safely standing.

Many are going to fall, but those who remain and abide in the Lord shall stand in the end. If you are the only one left standing, then **with thine eyes shalt thou behold and see the reward of the wicked.** That is what verse 8 goes on to say. You will see the wicked rewarded for their deeds. That doesn't mean that you shouldn't pray for them, but God is a just God, and the wicked man shall receive his reward.

No Evil Will Harm You
. . .

Verses 9 and 10 are the product of Moses' personal life and testimony. When he says, **Because thou hast made the Lord, which is my refuge, even the most High, thy habitation; there shall no evil befall thee, neither shall**

any plague come nigh thy dwelling, he means it. *No* evil will harm you, my friend. None! He isn't saying that evil won't ever come against you. But if you are a dweller in the secret place of the Most High, it won't ever overtake you. It won't succeed against you.

And not only are you promised divine defense, but if you are in fellowship with God, He extends an umbrella of protection over your family as well.

So how does God provide this formidable hedge of protection from harm? The next two verses give us the answer: **For he shall give his angels charge over thee, to keep thee in all thy ways. They shall bear thee up in their hands, lest thou dash thy foot against a stone** (Psalm 91:11,12).

God provides His protection and direction through the ministry of angels. This is their created purpose. No matter how many obstacles the enemy puts in your path, no matter how many stones he throws at you to keep you from your divinely appointed destiny, you will rise above them super-naturally. The angels will help you do that by keeping you in all your ways.

AND YOU WILL TREAD UPON THE ENEMY
• • •

This hedge of protection gives you the ability to run roughshod over the enemy. Verse 13 puts it this way, **Thou shalt tread upon the lion and adder: the young lion and the dragon shalt thou trample under feet.** The lion, adder and dragon are all metaphors for Satan. He is the roaring lion who is seeking someone to devour with reckless strength and boldness. (1 Peter 5:8.) He is the adder or old serpent in the Garden of Eden that made a stealthy, poisonous attack on the human race. And he is the dragon that will be cast into the bottomless pit by an angel according to the book of Revelation. (Revelation 20:2,3.)

All three of these animals depict the nature of the attacks of the enemy. And this verse says you will trample those enemies under your feet if you are in fellowship with the Lord.

The last three verses of this remarkable chapter are a prophetic summary. They are words spoken by God Himself as He directly addresses the one who abides in Him. First of all, He says, **Because he hath set his love upon me, therefore will I deliver him: I will set him on high, because he hath known my name** (v. 14). This verse underscores once more the idea of fellowship. The use of phrases such as, **Because he hath set his love upon me** and **because he hath known my name** portray a deep level of intimacy and connectedness. When we have that kind of fellowship, we are promised divine deliverance. We will be set up on high, which could imply an increased visibility and influence in our communities and businesses.

Then in verse 15, God goes on to say, **He shall call upon me, and I will answer him: I will be with him in trouble; I will deliver him, and honour him.** Again, we are promised deliverance in times of trouble and a swift answer when we call upon Him. Furthermore, He will give us success and bring honor to us.

Finally, verse 16 gives us the marvelous promise of long life when it says, **With long life will I satisfy him, and shew him my salvation.** In other words, you don't have to die until you are satisfied. If you reach seventy years of age, and you still aren't satisfied, then you can live on a while longer.

YOU ARE PROTECTED!

•••

Psalm 91 really is a remarkable psalm in that God promises to bring you and me divine protection through His angels when we are in fellowship with Him. Let's look at the kind of protection He promises us in this psalm one more time.

First, He says you are protected in the front. (v. 4.)

Then He says you are protected on the sides. (vv. 2,7.)

You are protected from behind. (vv. 4,11.)

You are protected on top or over you. (vv. 1,4.)

You are protected underneath. (vv. 12,13.)

You are protected day and night. (vv. 5,6,10.)

You are protected anywhere. (v. 11.)

And finally, His protection of you endures throughout this life and goes on into eternity. (v. 16.)

Personally, I think this psalm covers it all. You can't ask for more protection than that! But remember, these things are only for those who abide in the Lord and live in fellowship with Him.

There is no question about it. Qualifying for the promises listed in Psalm 91 will take some effort on your part. It will involve laying down some worldly weights and picking up some heavenly habits. But the Bible guarantees you that your efforts will be rewarded because you will enjoy the sweetest communion this life can offer, and you will release all the power of heaven's hosts to work on your behalf.

So if you haven't already, make the decision now to be one of those blessed ones who dwells in the secret place of the Most High, and determine that from here on out, you will make your relationship with Him *the number-one priority* of your life. When you do that, you will find yourself experiencing God's divine deliverance and protection including the supernatural ministry of His angels on your behalf—all the days of your life.

Endnotes
• • •

Chapter 1

1. Wall Street Journal, January 30, 1996, p. A8.

2. Merrill F. Unger, *Unger's Bible Dictionary* (Chicago: Moody Press, 1966), p. 578.

3. Wall Street Journal, January 30, 1996, p. A8.

Chapter 2

1. Darby, *The Holy Scriptures, A New Translation from the Original Languages.* (Sussex, England: A. J. Holman Company, 1975).

Chapter 3

1. W. E. Vine, *An Expository Dictionary of Biblical Words* (New York: Thomas Nelson, 1985), p. 411.

2. Nelson Sousa, "Ten Precious Minutes," *Guideposts Magazine*, December 1984, pp. 6-9.

3. Ann Cannady, "The Angel Came On Wednesday," *Guideposts Magazine*, May 1994, pp. 14-16.

Chapter 5

1. David Moore, "His Mysterious Ways," *Guideposts Magazine*, February, 1991, p. 29.

Chapter 6

1. Alfred Edersheim, *Bible History: Old Testament*, (Grand Rapids Michigan: William B. Eerdman's Publishing Co.), pp. vii, 144.

2. Ibid: p. 145.

Chapter 9

1. James Strong, *The Exhaustive Concordance of the Bible* (McLean: MacDonald, 1978), "Hebrew and Chaldee Dictionary of the Old Testament," p. 118, #8085.

2. W. E. Vine, *An Expository Dictionary of Biblical Words*, (New York: Thomas Nelson, 1985), p. 154.

Chapter 10

[1] W. E. Vine, *An Expository Dictionary of Biblical Words* (New York: Thomas Nelson, 1985), p. 316.

Chapter 11

[1] Francis Brown, *A Hebrew and English Lexicon of the Old Testament* (Oxford University Press, Oxford London, New York), pp. 1062, 96.

[2] Ibid, p. 224.

[3] Finis Jennings Dake, *Dake's Annotated Reference Bible* (Lawrenceville, Georgia: Dake Bible Sales, 1963), OT p. 1-1.

[4] James Strong, *The Exhaustive Concordance of the Bible* (McLean: MacDonald, 1978), "Hebrew and Chaldee Dictionary of the Old Testament," p. 32, #1966.

[5] Finis Jennings Dake, *Dake's Annotated Reference Bible* (Lawrenceville, Georgia: Dake Bible Sales, 1963), OT, pp. 63-3.

[6] Ibid., NT p. k-m 283-1.

[7] Ibid., OT p. a 6-4.

Chapter 13

[1] W. E. Vine, *An Expository Dictionary of Biblical Words* (New York: Thomas Nelson, 1985), p. 64.

[2] James Strong, *The Exhaustive Concordance of the Bible* (McLean: MacDonald Publishing, 1978), "Greek Dictionary of the New Testament," p. 65, #4268.

[3] Merrill F. Unger, *Unger's Bible Dictionary* (Chicago: Moody Press, 1966), p. 380.

[4] James Strong, *The Exhaustive Concordance of the Bible* (McLean: MacDonald Publishing, 1978), "Hebrew and Chaldee Dictionary of the Old Testament," p. 32, #1942 and p. 29, #1698.

[5] Merrill F. Unger, *Unger's Bible Dictionary* (Chicago: Moody Press, 1966), p. 380.

[6] Ibid., pp. 90,91.

[7] Ibid., p. 90.

[8] Ibid., pp. 90-91.

[9] Ibid., p. 90.

About the Author

Mac Hammond is founder and Senior Pastor of Living Word Christian Center, a large and growing church in Minneapolis, Minnesota.

Mac Hammond graduated from VMI (Virginia Military Institute) in 1965 with a Bachelor's degree in English with pre-law emphasis. Between 1970 and 1980, Mac Hammond was involved in varying capacities in the general aviation industry, including ownership of a successful aircargo business serving the Midwestern United States. A business merger brought the Hammonds to Minneapolis where they ultimately founded Living Word Christian Center in 1980.

Today, the ministries that spring from Living Word include Maranatha Christian Academy, a fully-accredited, pre-K through 12 Christian School; Living Word Recovery Services, a licensed out-patient treatment facility for chemical dependency; Living Word Bible Institute; and, of course, the national and international media outreach of Mac Hammond Ministries, which includes a weekly, one-hour television broadcast called *The Winners Way with Mac Hammond,* seen nationwide; a daily 60-second television commentary called *The Winner's Minute;* and a bimonthly magazine.

Mac has authored several internationally distributed books and is broadly acclaimed for his ability to apply the principles of the Bible to practical situations and the challenges of daily living.

To contact Mac Hammond, write to:

Mac Hammond • P.O. Box 29469 • Minneapolis, MN 55429

Please include your prayer requests and comments when you write.

Other Books by Mac Hammond

Angels at Your Service	*Positioned for Promotion*
Doorways to Deception	*Seeing and Knowing*
The Last Millennium	*Water, Wind, & Fire*

Additional copies of this book are
available from your local bookstore.

• HARRISON HOUSE • Tulsa, Oklahoma 74153

Prayer of Salvation

A born-again, committed relationship with God is the key to the victorious life. Jesus, the Son of God laid down His life and rose again so that we could spend eternity with Him in heaven and experience His absolute best on earth. The Bible says, "For God so loved the world, that he gave his only begotten Son, that whosoever believeth in him should not perish, but have everlasting life" (John 3:16).

It is the will of God that everyone receive eternal salvation. The way to receive this salvation is to call upon the name of Jesus and confess Him as your Lord. The Bible says, "That if thou shalt confess with thy mouth the Lord Jesus, and shalt believe in thine heart that God hath raised him from the dead, thou shalt be saved. For whosoever shall call upon the name of the Lord shall be saved" (Romans 10:9-10,13).

Jesus has given salvation, healing and countless benefits to all who call upon His name. These benefits can be yours if you receive Him into your heart by praying this prayer:

Heavenly Father, I come to You admitting that I am a sinner. Right now, I choose to turn away from sin, and I ask You to cleanse me of all unrighteousness. I believe that Your Son, Jesus died on the cross to take away my sins. I also believe that He rose again from the dead so that I might be justified and made righteous through faith in Him. I call upon the name of Jesus Christ to be the Savior and Lord of my life. Jesus, I choose to follow You, and ask that You fill me with the power of the Holy Spirit. I declare that right now, I am a born-again child of God. I am free from sin, and full of the right-eousness of God. I am saved in Jesus' name, Amen.

If you have prayed this prayer to receive Jesus Christ as your Savior, or if this book has changed your life, we would like to hear from you. Please write us at:

Harrison House Publishers • P.O. Box 35035 • Tulsa, Oklahoma 74153

You can also visit us on the web at www.harrisonhouse.com

The Harrison House Vision

Proclaiming the truth and the power
Of the Gospel of Jesus Christ
With excellence;

Challenging Christians to
Live victoriously,
Grow spiritually,
Know God intimately.